Praise for Achieving a Brea......

"Achieving a Breakthrough Transformation" is an excellent book, which combines decades of pricing expertise with tried and tested coaching techniques to deliver a practical guide to business success. This book is a must read for anyone seeking an authentic resource for improving productivity. The book not only expands on the principles of peak performance; it exposes the requisite psychological mindset for attaining such performance. Whether one is a seasoned business executive or an aspiring entrepreneur, the principles encapsulated in this book are invaluable.

-   Ejike Eze, Ph.D.,
CEO, Emerald Consulting Group

Exceptional leaders understand and honor the significance of individuals. They actively engage with their team, ensuring every member has the chance to make meaningful contributions. Stephane Joanis and Raymond Perras exemplify this, recognizing their paramount duty as leaders to nurture their team's growth and unleash their full potential.

Their dedication to these principles shines through in their latest work, "Achieving a Breakthrough Transformation." This book heralds a new era. I wholeheartedly endorse it to anyone striving for unprecedented excellence and innovation.

-   Ambassador Aminu A. Wisdom,
Former Nigerian Ambassador to ECOWAS,
Founder, Strategic Facilitations International
Chief Knowledge Officer of Strategic Global Mentorship
Author, Publisher, Speaker, and Entrepreneur Extraordinaire

Achieving a Breakthrough Transformation

I was lucky enough to have had a front seat at seeing Stéphane develop and employ the strategies he outlines in "Achieving a Breakthrough Transformation" for multiple years at Thermo Fisher Scientific. What was evident about Stephane's approach to the corporate world, was that he deliberately cared about his colleagues, his customers and himself in equal measure. I recall many a conversation with Stephane focused on leadership and how best to navigate the complexities of corporate America with humility and kindness – a trait not commonly identified with the intense environment of a global company.

I can see how he has distilled those learnings and created a framework that is easily digestible and can be implemented by anyone who is willing to embrace positive change.

- Mauricio Senties,
Group Vice President, ATS Life Sciences

Times have changed, we all noticed and with so much outdated information circulating, trying to fix tomorrow's problems with yesterday's thinking is a strategy doomed for failure.

Stephane Joanis brings new strategic insights, packaged in a well thought structure that truly equips the reader with an innovative framework that leaves no stones unturned. Combining logic with the heart is the best way to face the journey ahead, achieving the needed transformation to attain excellence and Peak Performance in a balanced way.

Reading this book will change your trajectory and make you experience a faster breakthrough... Guaranteed.

- Francois Lupien,
Business Success, Sales and Mindset Coach,
HowToBecomeMore.com

"Achieving a Breakthrough Transformation" is a powerful guide for success in today's rapidly evolving business landscape. Stephane Joanis seamlessly merges decades of broad leadership experience with coaching techniques. The author offers a practical roadmap for success - the key word is "practical". What sets this book apart is its ability to blend timeless principles of peak performance with essential mindset shifts needed to achieve it.

Joanis's innovative framework and emphasis on human-centric leadership make this book a practical guide for anyone seeking excellence and innovation. Through clear language and relatable examples, readers are given techniques and tools to release old habits, adopt a winning mindset, and achieve their goals with newfound clarity and energy. Whether you have decades of experience as a successful executive or are a first time entrepreneur or anywhere in between, this book is an important 'tool' for those ready to embark on a journey of growth and achievement.

- Dr. Steve Drury,
President, Focused Directions LLC

Read this book if you are looking to transform your life and achieve higher level of performance. What may seem like a complex set of concepts is distilled one step at a time in simple fashion.

The author makes you feels as if he is talking to you, guiding you through a framework with examples and anecdotes that bring these concepts to life. When you embrace the concepts in this book, you will change your way of thinking, break through old habits, adopt a wining mindset and take action to achieve your goals with a lot less energy than you ever thought possible.

Savio Gadelha Jr.,
Founder, ServiceWise Solutions LLC

Achieving a Breakthrough Transformation

We owe it to ourselves to reach our fullest potential. Stephane's book provides a practical and easy to follow guide to attaining excellence in all aspects of life. The methodology prescribed has significantly benefitted me both professionally and personally.

- Michael Nemergut,
Vice President, Thermo Fisher Scientific (retired)

I wear so many hats I cannot count them all, always running several businesses at once, with different teams. I am able to do it all while remaining relaxed and focused because of the lessons found within these pages.

- Sylvain Rochon,
Serial Entrepreneur, Futurist, Author,
Award-Winning Visionary Leader 2024.

Achieving a Breakthrough Transformation

How to instill and nurture the mindset for Peak Performance™

Stéphane Joanis

with Raymond Perras

SJ Performance, LLC
100 Holly Hill Dr
Oakdale, PA 15071
United States

ISBN-13: 979-8-218-49115-4

Cover design and illustrations by Stéphane Joanis

Achieving a Breakthrough Transformation

Acknowledgement

I want to thank my mother, Aline Joanis, and late father Roger Joanis who have taught me my faith and influenced my values. You are true examples of Proffective™ leadership.

Thank you to my mentors in relational marketing: André Blanchard, Brian Herosian, and David Taylor who taught me how to build relationships and the gentle art of influence.

Thank you, Raymond Perras (Coach P), for coaching me over the years and teaching me how to live excellence through Peak Performance™ with the right stuff in the right amount at the right time™ (Pace. . . Pace. . . Pace.).

The concept of Effort-*Less* Effectiveness™ through the book have been borrowed from Coach P's book "AïM for Life Mastery™." He has kindly agreed to have it enhance our discourse on Peak Performance™ so that you immediately start thinking about a transformation of your mindset.

Thank you to my wife, Josephine, for being my greatest supporter and cheerleader along the journey. Thank you for being my best friend and the best partner in life I could have chosen to raise Marvin, Amaka and Liam. I love you.

Finally, I thank you God for all the blessings that have molded me to become who I am.

Table of Contents

Foreword
By Aminu Amen Wisdom

The collaboration between these two eminent leaders yields a compelling instrument poised to shape our advancing era. This transformative work is a beacon for growth across all human pursuits.

As a seasoned author myself, I am enthralled by the insights shared by Stephane Joanis and Raymond Perras in this collaborative endeavor. Their expertise leaves no room for doubt.

In an age dominated by AI, where human involvement wanes, the need for tangible, result-driven information is paramount. As I delved into the contents of this book, I found its insights both fascinating and practical, offering prescriptions for a myriad of challenges.

I wholeheartedly endorse this material to anyone seeking success and breakthroughs, whether in their professional or personal lives.

This book serves as a roadmap, guiding readers from mediocrity to greatness, ushering them into a realm of effectiveness and transformation. Remember, "The Future You Cannot Picture In A Book, You Will Not Feature."

How to read this book

This book is meant to initiate you to concepts of Peak Performance™ used by SJ Performance, LLC coaches who help people achieve greater results with greater efficiency and less stress. You may want to go to specific areas of the book to explore concepts that particularly touch you.

You are invited to make this book as much a source of references for your individual challenges, as a recipe that is structured, strategic, systematic, and scalable to accompany your journey to a breakthrough transformation to reach a state of Effort-*Less* Effectiveness™.

A breakthrough transformation is one that takes you and your team to the next level with improved results driven by people performing optimally together towards a goal with a common set of values. This transformation always begins with a leader deciding to achieve this transformation within himself to model the way for his team.

> *We must seek in ourselves the change we seek in the world.*
> **-Mahatma Gandhi**

I hope that, as you read this book, you will be inspired to deepen your understanding and do more research focusing on your individual aspirations for excellence. The names of people and the settings of some stories have been modified to protect their identity.

Each section of the book contains comments to initiate reflection, stories to highlight a point, key takeaways to summarize the materials and deeper reflections.

Comments to initiate reflection.

Points to ponder

Stories to highlight a point.

Stories

Key takeaways at the end of each section.

Key take aways

Reflections from the master coach

Reflections from our master coach

Italic text in bold green are reflections from Coach P, who I refer to as the master coach. He has over 30 years of coaching experience in initiating breakthrough transformations.

Here are a couple of interesting ways to read this book.

I encourage you to quickly read through the key takeaways at the end of each section. They will provide insights into the main points of the sections. You can then proceed through the book as you would with a buffet in a restaurant and select the areas of interest where you desire to focus your attention.

Another approach is to read through the reflections from the master coach which will bring to light wisdom acquired over years of helping people to become more effective with the principles of Peak Performance™.

Here is the first one:

Reference in this book to Effort-Less Effectiveness™ were borrowed from Coach P's book "AïM for Life Mastery™." It is aimed at anchoring the concept of "less work "as opposed to "no work" in becoming effective. If it is repeated enough times, you will start integrating the concept in your daily routine by the time you finish the book.

My Personal Journey

I have been blessed with many opportunities where I was surrounded by heart-centered leaders who served as heroes, mentors, and friends to influence my life to become a more compassionate leader.

Multiple experts will suggest that success is in large part attributed to attitude over aptitude. While one may agree or disagree on the exact percentages, I believe that it would be difficult to argue against the idea that the right process with the wrong attitudes will inevitably fail. Human potential is a formidable strength in any organization and ought to be recognized. The aim of this book is to provide a time-tested process that is meant to unleash this potential.

Moving beyond tactics

Most of my professional career was invested introducing and implementing global pricing strategies for a multi-billion-dollar company. I also managed product lines representing tens of millions of dollars, met with customers around the world to solve their problems with new product innovations, and participated in the development of many new instruments.

I began to draft this book with the intent of sharing my technical know-how focusing on strategies and tactics to use pricing as a lever to improve sales velocity and profitability.

As I progressed with my research on pricing, I had a growing feeling that I was missing something. Pricing books focused on strategies, systems, and processes without much attention to the human factor, the key ingredient to flawless execution. The only exception would be a few books with a chapter on psychological factors that drive people to buy what they buy.

Pricing is a niche at the heart of organizations with an impact across multiple functional groups. I have experienced the pricing function at operational and strategic levels, reporting to corporate, finance, marketing, and sales operations.

Over the years I have come to understand that my success was not the result of a position, or a particular system (I have applied strategies across more than a dozen ERP systems). Instead, it was the result of the gentle art of influence. Someone taking the lead to align various functional groups at all levels of the organization to reach a common goal.

As I reflected on my work, it begged the question. . . Why focus efforts to author a book on tactics that may be used in the wrong context, or at the wrong time, when the real key to success is attributable to breaking through old paradigms and aligning people to achieve better results?

Mark twain is quoted as saying *"Too much of anything is bad, but too much good whiskey is barely enough."*

I will simply state that pricing is not whiskey. [1]

A New Beginning
In 2022 I was guided by the universe to make a conscious decision to start my own business and share my leadership expertise acquired through business experiences, in relational marketing, global strategic pricing, product management, commercial finance, business intelligence, and market intelligence.

Raymond Perras (Coach P) a certified professional coach, and my personal coach for over two decades, introduced me to the

---

[1] A list of good reading on pricing tactics is offered at the end of this book.

Achieving a Breakthrough Transformation

concept of Effort-*Less* Effectiveness™ which I have embraced early in my life within the framework of Peak Performance™. He cheered for me at the news that I was starting my own business SJ Performance, LLC.

Michael Nemergut (Mike) retired as VP Global Commercial for Chemical Analysis at Thermo Fisher Scientific in late 2020 and called me in the spring of 2022 after seeing my website. He asked me to have a virtual coffee with him and then shared his interest in what I was doing. We had developed a good relationship working together in the past and I welcomed his expertise when he offered it on our second virtual coffee one month later.

In the fall of 2022, I introduced Mike to Coach P and welcomed both as associates of SJ Performance, LLC. We began to meet virtually on a weekly basis to create a brighter future making the world a better place.

We reviewed the vision and mission and values of SJ Performance, LLC. We then agreed on six fundamental values to function as our guardrails, established guiding principles to work together in the most efficient way and agreed to live by the model that we teach.

Witnessing Personal Transformation

As SJ Performance, LLC progressed, it became apparent that many of the concepts from Coach P's program were new to Mike. He embraced the concepts and enjoyed applying them in several aspects of his life towards experiential growth.

We began to see a transformation after six to eight weeks of conversation. He would share his new awareness of negative self-talk on the golf course. He would then recognize it in others and could point out limiting beliefs. He started guitar lessons

Achieving a Breakthrough Transformation

and began to progress rapidly with visualization exercises. He would use the concept on the golf course to win his golf club's championship in 2023.

I would witness a similar transformation in a client that I was also coaching in parallel. This client would transform from a position of pain with self-doubt to enjoying more moments of gratitude and peace while enjoying greater confidence.

As time progressed, while recognizing the value of our unique business skills, our team morphed to focus more on leadership and the growing need for leaders. We all recognized the power of Coach P's structured process to reach Effort-*Less* Effectiveness™.

In the summer of 2023, I made the decision to offer a leadership think-tank and apply the mastermind principle which I had learned when I was in my twenties. During the preparations, Coach P, brought up how he wanted to discuss heart-centered leadership during this program.

The discussions that followed were priceless as we reflected on the importance of heart-centered leadership and recognized it in ourselves and others. We reflected on how to help leaders rediscover the power of human potential with a focus on heart-centered leadership, which we believe to be a catalyst for transformational leadership. This led us to an improved vision to guide people to self-transformation in becoming heart-centered leaders.

Mike was so inspired by one of our discussions on heart-centered leadership that he asked for his title to be changed from commercial excellence coach to leadership coach.

The Need for Heart-Centered Leaders

The last few decades have been characterized by many technological advancements introduced with great velocity. Managers have access to more data than ever before with an influx of information that can be overwhelming when delivered without insights. Managers need to sift through more information to make their decisions. This pulls them further and further from the people that they are meant to lead.

The 2019 pandemic left a void and brought organizations to the brink as it forced human resource teams to fill management and leadership positions in a competitive labor market. The result was the promotion of many managers to fill both positions of management and leadership without the necessary formation and guidance.

Many managers were promoted to fill voids at higher levels based on their skills in managing processes and hitting their numbers. The reward reinforced their resulting beliefs that success is due to policies, systems, and processes, moving them further away from recognizing that any great achievement is the result of the human potential at play.

As such, there is an influx of managers in positions of leadership. The rising cost of living, wage stagnation, and hostile work conditions contributed to the Great Resignation, or Big Quit of 2021. As a result, more people were promoted to fill the voids. We foresee a growing crisis and need for heart-centered leadership.

In their "State of the Global Workplace: 2023 Report" Gallup reported that only 24% of employees strongly agree that their organization cares about their overall well-being. They also showed that 77% of U.S. employees are either quietly quitting or actively disengaged at work.

Achieving a Breakthrough Transformation

While the ability to manage structures and processes is important, leaders need to recognize their contribution in creating alignment within their organization to inspire individuals in the team toward reaching a greater vision and mission.

They can help create a pull by touching the human heart.

The value of following through

What if your favorite sports team announced that they were planning to reduce costs by getting rid of the coaching positions and managing the team without a coach? You probably could not imagine this team winning a championship. Professional sports teams operate at an elevated level of excellence and have identified and recognized the importance of a coach to their organization.

The concept of coaching is not new and has been demonstrated in business and in sports. Good coaches provide an opportunity to follow through with multiple touch points for the manager/leader to receive feedback as they assimilate new concepts and deal with new business problems. In short, it works.

In their book, The Peter Principle [2], Laurence J. Peter and Raymond Hull explain how business organizations often promote people to their level of incompetence because the recruiters make their decisions based on the talents and competencies related to the candidate's last position as opposed to the skills necessary for the new position.

---

[2] Laurence, R. H. H. P. D., & Peter, L. J. (2020). The Peter Principle: Why Things Always Go Wrong.

The leadership pipeline model provides the framework to help managers progress to new management levels with clear definitions or the different skill requirements, time applications and work values at each level. In other words, the new capabilities required to execute the new responsibilities, the new time frames that govern how one works, and what people believe is important and so becomes the focus of their efforts. [3]

My experience and research indicate that many businesses are failing to develop leadership bench strength and day-to-day effectiveness. Managers continue to be promoted based on a greater focus on past short-term financial results in a prior role over their personal soft skills and leadership skills at the new leadership level.

Most people see themselves filling a position rather than being part of a pipeline. When gaps are not addressed, it can prevent a manager from progressing on to the next level or at worst, clog up the leadership pipeline and lead to a demotion.

Leaders often find a point in their career where coaching from their manager is insufficient or non-existent because their manager does not see themselves as a coach or simply does not value coaching their direct reports as a priority over the day-to-day short-term operational goals.

So, why is it that some companies hire and promote managers/leaders and provide some training without follow-up, internally or from a professional coach to start on the right foot?

---

[3] Charan, R., Drotter, S., Noel, J., (2011) The Leadership Pipeline: How to build the leadership powered company, John Wiley & Sons, Inc.

Achieving a Breakthrough Transformation

Is it:

1. Misplaced ego with a belief that the best talent has been hired and that the best answers can only come from inside the box?
2. A lack of belief that the new manager/leader will provide a good return on the investment?
3. A lack of desire to seek excellence?
4. A corporate bottom line driven approach that omits to recognize that results are produced by people, not systems, policies, spreadsheets, or progress reports.
5. Or an omission due to lack of understanding of the role of a leader as opposed to the role of a manager.

Many companies will hire a motivational speaker for their annual kickoff meeting where everyone gets energized for a few days without following through on the concepts presented. Employees are sent back into their old routine with the same state of mind. No further action is taken towards achieving a long-term transformation.

Yet, to achieve a new level of awareness, there must be a breakthrough transformation: let go old values that provided success at lower levels of leadership but are no longer relevant and even detrimental in the new role.

The Peak Performance™ framework was introduced in sports and has led multiple professional athletes to reach breakthrough transformations to achieve extraordinary results. The same approach has also been used successfully in business.

We aspire to enable you to achieve Peak Performance™. You will learn the steps to shift old paradigms preventing you from progressing to new leadership levels and apply and integrate **your** new paradigms more efficiently to achieve a breakthrough transformation to Peak Performance™.

Achieving a Breakthrough Transformation

Personal testimony

The principles in this book have provided me with many opportunities and blessings. In early 2022 I wrote a thank you letter to my last employer (more about this topic later). In this letter I acknowledged gratitude for the following:

- Compassion in allowing me to continue assisting my mother with her business after my father passed away from Cancer when I was 23 years old.
- Flexibility enabling me to build my own business and grow a new organization of over 250 people in six months through relational marketing.
- The sponsorship of my family to become permanent residents of the United States.
- Support of the PMC-III certification with Pragmatic institute.
- Long-term and short-term incentive awards.
- Travel opportunities to fifteen countries around the world.
- Training on the practical process improvement (PPI).
- Training on the A3 process of managing to learn.
- Support for the adoption of our son.
- Sponsorship of my MBA which I completed at age 46.

Reflection on Stephane's insights:
Writing this letter enabled him to see the good side of what was happening. He developed the belief that, indeed, the universe was guiding his progress to excellence. Shifting and re-orienting his career was opening countless opportunities to achieve and share his discoveries. This book is a testimonial to his new mission in life.

I have been blessed with experiences that have enriched my life and made me a better man. I have learned many lessons from professional talented people with high skill levels in multiple fields.

Achieving a Breakthrough Transformation

I value the relationships and friendships that have been built over the years. I can honestly say that the journey has been transformative, and I am deeply grateful for the doors that it has opened to serve the world towards being a better place.

I decided to write this book and integrate the lessons learned from Coach P with lessons learned from my interactions with other heart-centered leaders, mentors and friends such as André Blanchard, a master in relational marketing [4]; Sijo Jacques Patenaude, a Kung Fu master [5]; Brian Herosian, a professional Canadian football player and entrepreneur; François Lupien, a trusted friend and life coach; Bill Britt, a business leader for hundreds of thousands; Rich Devos, founder of Amway, my father's hero, and a personal source of inspiration [6];

This book also includes a few lessons learned from my father who personally inspired thousands of people to grow and become better leaders. He provided me with a solid foundation to become a compassionate leader. I wish I could have enjoyed more years learning from him.

---

[4] Blanchard, A. (1992). Your financial freedom through network marketing. Saint-Hubert, Quebec: Éditions Un Monde différent.
[5] Patenaude, J., & Patenaude, J. (2000). One and Three Inch Power Punch: Unleash the Power Within. [Casselman, Ont.]: Fang Shen Do Pub.
[6] Devos, R. (2000). Hope from my heart: J. Countryman

Introduction

The purpose of this book is to introduce you to a process to instill and nurture the concepts of Peak Performance™ to achieve a state of Effort-*Less* Effectiveness™. While you may find that some of the ideas are not new, you will discover that they are organized towards achieving a breakthrough transformation with maximum effectiveness.

Many of the concepts presented in this book were learned through thirty years of interactions with Raymond Perras (Coach P) and with other leaders in various industries. Coach P is a certified performance coach who has perfected his recipe with many professional athletes to help them through breakthrough transformations to win championships. He has documented his personal approach in his book *AïM for Life Mastery™*. [7]

This book provides additional insights focused on achieving a breakthrough transformation through a structured process that is structured, strategic, systematic, and scalable to align your mind and body to channel your efforts in a single direction in a way that is efficient to maximize the results that you want. We invite you to this strategic journey to excellence.

Tiers of competency

Each of us has different interests that pull us to explore different specific skills. In some cases, we become proficient to the point of mastery where we do not have to think about what we are doing anymore. This is where you would be said to have

---

[7] Perras, R. (2011). AïM for Life Mastery™: A Process That Will Empower You to Create Your Chosen Level of Performance While Reducing Stress.

reached a level of unconscious competence which we refer to as a state of Effort-*Less* Effectiveness™.

There comes a time where you may want to share your skills to enable others to progress with greater velocity. Teaching these skills requires bringing them back into consciousness to relearn and reframing your existing knowledge to use it more effectively.

The activity of walking is a good example. One of my clients, a certified Rolfer, helps people rediscover their mobility by engaging the relationship between their internal space and external environment. One example of the power that can be gained from bringing skills back to consciousness is how people use Rolfing to draw and engage respect from their colleagues by owning their presence and stepping into their space.

The tiers of competency model refers to the levels of expertise that an individual can achieve in a particular skill or task. The outer circle of this model divides our competencies into three levels: novice, intermediate, and expert.

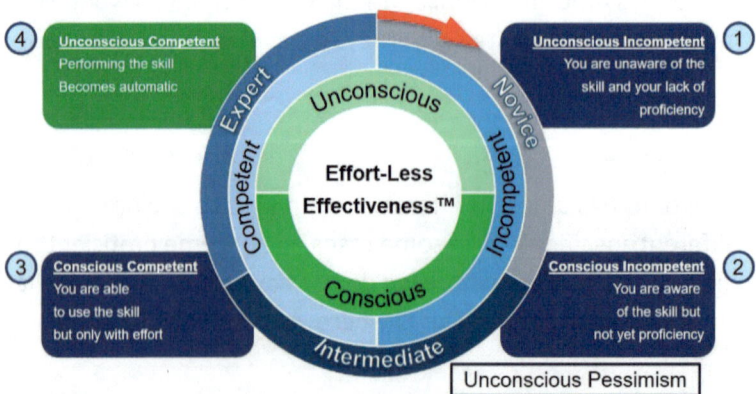

Each tier of competency requires distinct levels of dedication and commitment. Progressing to the next level requires continuous effort to improve skills and knowledge.

Achieving a Breakthrough Transformation

NOTE: if you stop and think about your life experiences, every activity, lesson, discovery, adaptation, learning, applying, muddling through, all began and ended or are progressing along that journey to unconscious competence.

Novice

Novice expertise is the stage where a person is just starting to learn a new skill or concept. A person is unconsciously incompetent, meaning they are unaware of how little they know or understand about the subject. As they continue to learn, they become aware of their lack of knowledge which is known as conscious incompetence. This is the first step to self-improvement as new awareness of the missing skills and knowledge enables a person to take steps for strategic improvement.

Intermediate

Intermediate expertise is a stage of learning that bridges conscious incompetence and conscious competence. It is a stage in which the learner has begun to understand the basics of the skills or knowledge he or she is trying to acquire but is still far from mastering them.

Moving up to the next level of competence requires you to be mindful, intentional, and present. This involves recognizing one's own gaps and actively working to fill them in a more deliberate and conscious way. It is also a crucial point where people are often unconsciously pessimistic. Where many decisions are made to either abandon improving the skill or double down to master them with additional efforts.

The individual must gain a deeper understanding of the concepts and be able to apply their knowledge in a more sophisticated manner. As they progress, they will become consciously competent, where they are able to apply their knowledge and skills with greater confidence.

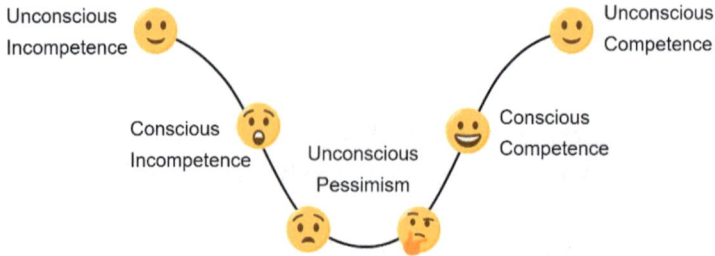

Expert

Expert skill is the result of competence that is ingrained into the routine. Conscious competence involves the individual's ability to understand, analyze, and apply the knowledge and skills they have acquired with conscious effort and deliberate practice.

A higher level of competence follows as our abilities improve to the point that we perform skills or tasks without conscious thought (on automatic). This is achieved through repetitive practice, which leads to the development of "muscle memory" and an unconscious understanding of the material. To achieve expert skill (expertise), a person must first become consciously competent in their chosen field and then build upon this knowledge through repetition and practice to develop unconscious competence to peak performance™.

Peak performance is a state of Effort-*Less* Effectiveness™ reached when a person has practiced enough times that they can perform the task well under pressure. They move past "thinking" to become "instinctive" in their delivery. They trust in their abilities and do not have to struggle to achieve results which seem to come by themselves as the result of repetition and practice.

Success at this level is not about working hard and pushing the limits but having built a high operating threshold that allows us to operate with ease where others would stumble.

Unconscious competence is the basic tenet of being in the ZONE or operating in FLOW. It relates directly to a STATE of mind that ensures excellence on a sustained basis.

The Transform*Action*™ Framework

The Transform*Action*™ framework was first illustrated by Raymond Perras (Coach P) and contains the elements of the journey to a Breakthrough Transformation.

Achieving optimal results with minimal effort requires an approach that is structured, strategic, systematic, and scalable. This framework addresses the mind, body, and soul.

©Copyright Raymond Perras 2022

Each is a dimension of the personal transformation that you will experience as you learn the concept of "Easy to understand, easy to apply, easy to measure."

Achieving a Breakthrough Transformation

The framework serves as a guide to continuous improvement from the inside out. The various elements help to build an approach that leads to Effort-*Less* Effectiveness™. You will gain mastery of your natural tendency to worry and learn to redirect your energy toward your desired goals. The greatest benefit in your overall capabilities and capacities is reduced stress.

As you have a whole lifetime of learning and discovery behind you, you must believe that who you are now is the result of all your life experiences. It did not happen overnight.

Similarly, the personal transformation you will experience as you journey through these concepts and ideas will take time to understand and apply. Be patient and persistent. Your aspirations of achieving peak performance in all you do will be fulfilled. Just take it one day at a time. Keep your focus on the process. As the Nike's motto says, "Just Do It!"

This book focuses on honing your internal powers to achieve more with less stress. The concepts are presented within a circular framework to express the never-ending nature of the pursuit of excellence.

The outer ring represents the three pillars of your inner power. It is the foundation that leads to self-responsibility to create excellence in everything you do.

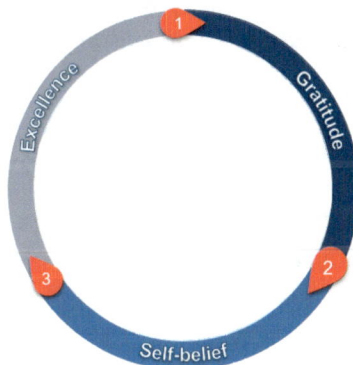

Achieving a Breakthrough Transformation

As with any ingrained capability, these pillars will be reinforced daily to ensure vitality, availability, and integration into who you are. They form an indestructible launch pad that supports all your efforts to maximize results while reducing stress.

The middle ring identifies the pathways to continuous improvement necessary to achieve Peak Performance.

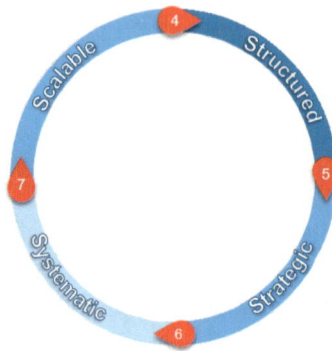

Continuous improvement is about seeking to be better every day in one area of activity. As Tom Peters once said, "Better achieve the thousand one percenters than the two or three one hundred percenters."

"I fear not the man who has practiced 10,000 kicks once, but I fear the man who has practiced one kick 10,000 times."

-Bruce Lee

The premise of continuous improvement addresses small steps repeated consistently. It is founded on three characteristics: uniform (structured), consistent (strategic) and repeatable (systematic). As we learn to do "continuous improvement," the behavior becomes scalable, that is "transferable" to all aspects of our lives.

Achieving a Breakthrough Transformation

The inner circle provides a structured approach with the technique by which top performers integrate body and mind in a dance to produce excellence as a habit.

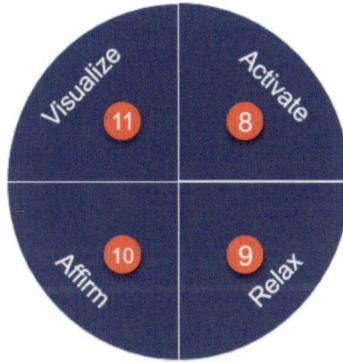

The best illustration of the application of Activate/Relax/Affirm/Visualize is the preparation for an athletic event by an Olympic athlete. Those four actions are integrated into their routine every day so that their state (mindset, etc.) is focused on achieving excellence.

Everyone seeking to be their best self will benefit from consistent practice of this mental gym activity.

A Structured Approach

We will go through the framework from the outer ring to the inside in a way that is intuitive and sequential to allow the reader to apply and integrate the concepts with maximum effectiveness.

This book does not focus on the inner diamond which highlights the seven pathways of the Transform*Action*™ process. These steps will be covered in a separate book to help you achieve your vision more effectively after you have achieved the first part of the breakthrough transformation process that permanently shifts your mindset to a capacity and capability that is based on mastery gained through continuous and sustained practice – the Mental Gym.

TransformAction™
Vision
Mission
Values
Funnel
Leadership
Focus
Communication

This concept originated from our master coach, Coach P, in his coaching practice. It is an approach that has enabled numerous people, including myself, to achieve beyond expectations by using their innate capabilities to create successful outcomes.

You will learn the internal power that you possess within your mind to create an environment that will allow you to prioritize time for thinking and reflection towards advancing towards your purpose. You will learn the importance of tapping your M.I.P.™ (being mindful, intentional, and present) to be at the top of your game when performing.

The upwards journey within an organization requires that people acquire a new way of managing and leading skill requirements, time applications, and work values and leave the old ways behind. [8] In essence, a leader that is moving upwards

---

[8] Charan, R., Drotter, S., Noel, J., (2011) The Leadership Pipeline: How to build the leadership powered company, John Wiley & Sons, Inc.

must go through numerous breakthrough transformations. The ability to recognize and adjust to a new set of values and achieve mastery with velocity will determine the altitude that one can reach.

The law of inertia

Newton's First Law of Motion states that an object in motion tends to stay in motion unless an external force acts upon it. Similarly, if the object is at rest, it will remain at rest unless an unbalanced force acts upon it. In the same way, working and moving towards reaching a higher level of effectiveness will require effort and, once in motion, it will become easier to stay in the motion towards reaching Effort-Less Effectiveness™. It is like a plane that uses most of its fuel as it climbs to reach its cruising altitude. Once it has reached it, it requires very little effort to remain there.

Achieving a Breakthrough Transformation

Unleashing your potential

Unleashing your potential involves taking responsibility for your results. It starts by working on what is inside you. In a few words, finding your own inspiration so that you may inspire others to be the best they can be.

We aspire to help you achieve an increased awareness of old paradigms that you should let go. We will challenge you and assist you in reframing your mindset with new affirmations that will tap into your subconscious mind so that it can serve you better to recognize new opportunities where you can shine and achieve beyond your wildest expectations.

We want to inspire you to elevate your mindset with gratitude and increased self-belief that will enable you to overcome greater challenges, have access to more opportunities, and rise to a higher state of Effort-*Less* Effectiveness™ for maximum results.

We want to help you reach Peak Performance™; to apply the right stuff, in the right amount, at the right time™ to get better results while reducing your efforts.

Do not just read this book for the sake of reading. Use it as a guide. Take the time to apply the principles and do the exercises in the order they are presented, and you will feel, see, and achieve a transformation to a state of focused energy in the direction of your goals.

On your Mark . . .

GrativatE™ is about building a solid foundation that gives you stability to weather any storms that may come our way. It is important to invest time to strategically reflect on our foundation, our mind and spirit, and our character to build the strength and conviction that will allow us to stay true to our values, to make wise decisions, and to stay motivated to reach our goals.

We use the word GrativatE™ to describe the process to embrace gratitude, elevate your mind to Instill self-belief, and seek Excellence. As you progress in this book, you will learn how gratitude and self-belief are the foundation of a successful mindset in the pursuit of excellence.

Our objective as coaches is to provide a greater awareness to areas where we are preventing ourselves from achieving and recognizing the positive moments in life, to appreciate the people and situations that have contributed to reaching this present moment of self-discovery.

It does not matter if you are experiencing some level of success and wanting to reach new heights or going through a slump that you are seeking to put behind you. Know that you did not stumble on this book by random chance and that you can "will" your mind to move on to the next challenges. We offer this book to provide you with a framework to be the best that you can be as you seek excellence in all aspects of life in the pursuit of achievement.

> **"Every day, in every way, I am getting better and better."**
> **-Emile Coué**

You are about to go through a breakthrough transformation by embracing gratitude and instilling self-belief in a way that will prepare you to make the decision to seek excellence.

You are the architect of your future, and your future starts now.

"I have what it takes to succeed and be happy.

Yesterday does not dictate how today will be.
I choose to make today better than yesterday.
Tomorrow will be better than today.

The best of me is enough."
                                        -Stéphane Joanis

GrativatE™

GrativatE™ represents the work we must perform on ourselves to facilitate the journey to a breakthrough transformation. It reflects the shift in focus from negative to positive outlook by being grateful for the many blessings in our life. It indicates the internal focus on all the skills, knowledge and abilities accumulated in a lifetime that form the foundation of self-belief. We are unique, special and no one is exactly like us.

Ultimately, aim is the key to achieving, or hitting the mark. So, our waking moments should strive to reach excellence (the E) and be the best at what we do.

> *"It is better to shoot for the stars and hit the top of a post than to aim for the top of a post and shoot yourself in the foot."*
> **- Unknown**

Embrace Gratitude, Instill Self-Belief, and Seek Excellence

We suggest that the three pillars of internal power and self-actualization aim at setting a positive tone, going inside oneself and recognizing acquired strengths, and working tirelessly to implement excellence in what you do. Self-satisfaction is gained when we give everything we have to give.

Practice leaving it on the field, as famous football coach Vince Lombardi taught his players.

Building a foundation

Our internal power is a continuum and the foundation of all human action in the breakthrough transformation process. This process is driven from the inside and requires awareness of our acquired skills, abilities, experiences, and knowledge.

However, this awareness must be actioned through internalization to conscious knowledge, and integration into proactive actions that help transform behaviors. Awareness only becomes useful when repetition transforms the awareness into habits that produce peak performance.

My father would compare the process of achieving in life to building a house. The foundation corresponds to our mind and spirit which are guided by our values. It is essential to build a good foundation if you want to reach your goals in a sustainable way. Even if built with the greatest intentions, a house on a poor foundation is bound to collapse over time.

The walls represent the structure, strategy, and scalable systems to support the roof. They enable you to progress towards your goals and provide hope to achieve them.

Embrace Gratitude, Instill Self-Belief, and Seek Excellence

It is important to note that the roof represents the achievement of dreams and aspirations as an outcome. The initial vision that leads to reaching your dreams and aspirations belongs in the mind and spirit. The only limit to how big and how high the roof will be is in your mind.

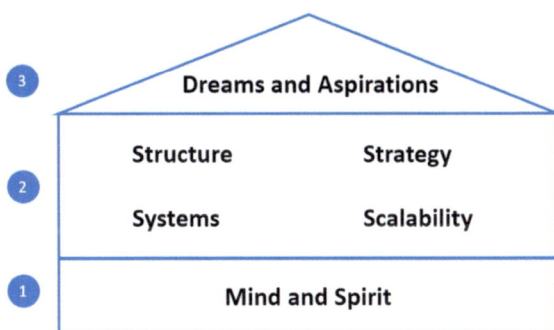

The analogy of a house being built is suggested to illustrate how setting a weak foundation leaves the stability and robustness of the action in a fragile state. Unexpected obstacles or accidents can blow the whole structure down – the same applies to human beings striving to achieve with a shaky foundation as support.

We believe that a journey begins with a starting point and a destination. It is important to take inventory of where we are emotionally before determining where we want to go in the future.

Get Ready to GrativatE™ as we dive into the internal powers that form the foundation to achieve Effort-*Less* Effectiveness™.

When you decide to achieve your goals, you get the right information and apply it to produce the desired results. It all happens inside!

Success is an inside job, and the feeling of success is achieved when actions are aligned with your WHY. It is not about the position that you are in, but about the direction towards which you are going. Just like when you navigate a boat, if you are going in the wrong direction, you can always change course. The choice is yours!

Gratitude

Gratitude is the first pillar of internal power enabling a focus on the positive aspects of our lives and the world around us.

"When you meet obstacles with gratitude, your perception starts to shift, resistance loses its power, and grace finds a home within you."

- Oprah Winfrey

Striving to focus on the "good" and being grateful helps to rewire our subconscious brain to see the positive side of things. In the end, being grateful as a first reaction liberates our capability to create and design solutions with less effort.

There is something magical about a positive state of mind. It has to do with a positive bias that shifts our outlook from negative to positive. Focusing on gratitude opens our eyes to the good side of things and allows us to be creative in finding ways to improve or correct a situation. We therefore suggest building the habit of seeking gratitude through practice.

The antidote to fear

Gratitude is an antidote to fear. It helps to put fear into perspective, as we can recognize that there are many things to

Embrace Gratitude, Instill Self-Belief, and Seek Excellence

be thankful for, and that fear is only a small part of our experience.

Our upbringing has been full of negative prods from parents, teachers, adults coaching us, mentors or even superiors in later years who have said "NO" or some other negation of our actions or thinking in providing well-meaning feedback. Over the years, we thus have been programmed to focus on the negative as a first knee jerk reaction. No wonder we tend to be initially negative when faced with an issue.

> *"During the first eighteen years of our lives, if we grew up in fairly average, reasonably positive homes, we were told "No!," or that we could not do, more than 148,000 times!"[9]*
> - **Dr. Shad Helmstetter**

I like to say, "It's magic!" Embracing gratitude enables us to decrease the power of fear and empowers us to move progressively to Effort-Less Effectiveness™.

When we are in a state of gratitude, we are enabled to focus on the positive aspects of our lives and the world around us. This encourages us to be mindful of the abundance in our lives and the world, helping us to recognize that there is always something positive to focus on and that our fears are not insurmountable. By embracing gratitude, we can learn to recognize our fears and find ways to move forward with courage and resilience.

Gratitude enables the "PULL" to act effectively to help us land at a new level of excellence. Without it, we are driven to a negative outlook that makes us prisoners of our worries and fears and drives us into the negative spiral of helplessness.

---

[9] Helmstetter, S. (2017). What to say when you talk to your self. Simon and Schuster.

Embrace Gratitude, Instill Self-Belief, and Seek Excellence

Forgiveness as a Twin to Gratitude

Forgiveness is a conscious decision to release negative energy in the form of feelings and thoughts towards someone who has hurt you. It is an act of self-care and self-love, and it is an important part of healing and creating a healthy life. It is a process of letting go of the hurt and anger and choosing to move forward instead of dwelling on the past. By forgiving, you are not condoning the wrongs that were committed, but instead choosing to focus on the present and the future.

Forgiveness and gratitude go hand in hand. When we forgive, we let go of any resentment we have and open ourselves up to being grateful for what we have. Without forgiveness we hold on to negative emotions and give the person who has wronged us power over our emotions. The energy spent on these negative feelings limits us from embracing our full potential by focusing our energy on our goals.

Resentment is like a poison that you drink, then hope that the other person will die. The only person who gets hurt is YOU!

The decision to put the past behind you and focus on who you want to be in the future is entirely yours. No one benefits from feeling sorry for themselves, or for the things that they have done in the past and cannot undo. Free yourself by forgiving others and, more importantly, forgiving yourself.

Charity

Giving back is an act that is not only beneficial for the receiver but also the donor. It uplifts the spirit, helps us build self-confidence, allows us to focus on helping others and invites abundance in our own life. When we are grateful for the abundance in our life and at peace with ourselves, we create a positive spiral that attracts more blessings. It helps us detach from material things so that we can focus on the important things.

The self-satisfaction of giving is more wholistically beneficial to the person giving than to the reward for the receiver. The spirit is lifted by giving and focusing on others.

My wife was born in Nigeria where millions of people live without basic drinking water or electricity. Our children were tasked to bring some of their toys when they were around 8 years old so that they could experience the joy of giving. The experience of giving their toys to a Nigerian child was positively impactful for each of them.

Gratitude towards your team

The success of any project or organization is heavily dependent on the efforts and contributions of the team members. By acknowledging and expressing gratitude for their hard work and dedication, you not only boost their morale and motivation, but also foster a sense of unity and camaraderie within the team and this builds trust.

Furthermore, expressing gratitude towards your team can also have a positive impact on your own leadership skills. It helps you to recognize and appreciate the strengths and talents of each team member, allowing you to delegate tasks more effectively and build a stronger, more efficient team.

A grateful attitude leads to a culture of appreciation and positivity within your team, for increased productivity in a work environment that is more enjoyable for everyone.

Possibility thinking

A positive attitude and a free spirit allow the mind to open up to possibility thinking towards achieving our dreams. In his book, "Move Ahead with Possibility Thinking" [10] Robert Schuller encouraged people to develop a positive outlook on life by recognizing and embracing the potential for success in every situation. The book emphasized the importance of taking risks, facing challenges, and learning from mistakes, and encourages readers to focus on what is achievable rather than what is not.

---

[10] Schuller, R. (1977). Move ahead with possibility thinking.

Embrace Gratitude, Instill Self-Belief, and Seek Excellence

IDEAS TO INCREASE GRATITUDE

Gratitude Journal

Start a daily gratitude journal and write down three things you are grateful for each day. This exercise helps to shift your focus to the positive and can help you to appreciate the trivial things in life.

Gratitude Visit

Take a trip to visit someone you are grateful for and tell them why you are thankful for them. This exercise helps to express your gratitude to someone directly and can help to strengthen relationships.

Gratitude Meditation

Take a few minutes to sit in silence and focus on the things you are grateful for in your life. This exercise helps to bring a sense of peace and can help to reduce stress.

Gratitude Letter

Write a letter to someone you are grateful for and tell them why you appreciate them. This exercise helps to express your gratitude in a meaningful way and can help to strengthen relationships.

Gratitude Reading

Og Mandino's book "The greatest miracle in the world which includes "the Memorandum from God. . . to You." It is an inspiring story that uplifts the spirit and increases awareness of the miracles around us.

Embrace Gratitude, Instill Self-Belief, and Seek Excellence

Key take aways

- The GrativatE™ process represents embracing gratitude, instilling self-belief, and seeking excellence.
- An attitude of gratitude is an antidote to fear as it allows us to focus on positives.
- Forgiveness and charity are acts that help to free and uplift the spirit. They enable gratitude to take root more easily.
- A spirit that is free from resentment and blame frees the mind to think positively.
- Positive thinking raises awareness of possibilities, bringing them into focus.
- Free yourself from the past; forgive others and yourself.
- Generosity uplifts the spirit, gives us greater peace, and attracts positive abundance.

Stop "just reading."

If you have not taken a note, made a call, or taken a single pause to reflect on an area that you are grateful for, then you are "just reading."

Self-belief

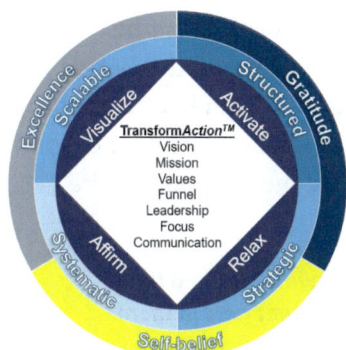

As the second pillar of internal power, self-belief is a mission critical element of the concept of "capability."

Just like gratitude liberates our desires to achieve, self-belief anchors our internal power to act. If we lack self-belief, we lack belief in our own capabilities; there will be times when obstacles or barriers to achievement will overwhelm us. Personal power comes from our inner strength to face challenges and find ways to overcome them.

Lack of self-belief will lead to a "Give up" attitude. Often, when we are faced with such a situation, we will tend to remember other times when effort was futile. Self-belief can be an antidote for those moments.

The root of your self-belief lies in your past successes, achievements, and times you have overcome. Taking inventory of past successes is an exercise that will automatically shift your thinking to a "Can do - Will do" attitude. Remind yourself that you have what it takes to get through the challenge. It is key to seeking excellence; better today than yesterday, even if it is just a little bit better. Success breeds success.

> *The extraordinary is achieved in doing a little extra every day.*
> *- Stéphane Joanis*

Embrace Gratitude, Instill Self-Belief, and Seek Excellence

Self-belief is intricately linked to the core of human potential. As a sandcastle cannot withstand wind or rain, low self-belief gets bowled over when obstacles or barriers, imaginative or real, appear in our road to accomplishment. We can have visions of grandeur, hope of wonderful success, a wish to achieve beyond expectations. If our self-belief is weak, the outcome will be much less than imagined.

> *Ships don't sink because of the water around them;*
> *Ships sink because of the water that gets in them.*
> *Don't let what's happening around you get inside you*
> *and weigh you down.*
> - Unknown

Similarly, the negativity of the world cannot put you down unless you allow it to get inside you.

Beware helplessness! Digging deep into your past achievements builds self-belief and provides the impetus to move with inner strength toward overcoming any obstacle that lies in the path to your success.

Vern and Clyde

Let us examine two fictitious characters, Vern and Clyde, to examine the concepts that will serve to instill self-belief. You could say that Vern and Clyde are twins as they look the same on the surface, except for one difference.

Vern   Clyde

Vern is grateful for his past, enjoys the present and looks forward to an even better future. He is a positive person with a great self-image, he sees himself as a leader, he his courageous, he sets ambitious goals with no fear of missing them, takes risks that allow him to learn new skills, is provided with more opportunities that he welcomes and uses to learn new skills.

Each challenge is like a steppingstone to another opportunity. He strives to do what is right, is grateful for the people around him, seeks excellence and is respected by people who surround him.

Clyde is troubled by his past; he compares himself to others and struggles to see how he could be as talented as others. He does not set goals in general, and when he does, the goals are modest out of fear of missing them as he aims for perfection which is evading him.

Embrace Gratitude, Instill Self-Belief, and Seek Excellence

He goes through challenges with difficulty, with each of them being an obstacle to his success. He remembers people who have disappointed him and questioning if he can trust the next people he meets in life. He is guarded, feels that feedback is a judgment against him and doubts his ability to benefit from the feedback.

Vern and Clyde may have gone through the same challenges in life. They may have had an abusive father, been neglected in their childhood, lived in poverty and none of these experiences would explain their different perspective. Vern processed these experiences as steppingstones that reinforced his character while Clyde would use them as obstacles preventing him from progressing and succeeding.

This story illustrates our power to interpret and justify most anything. Adding meaning to experiences goes a long way to create a launching pad to increase performance, or an anchor that stops us in our tracks. The choice is always ours.

Everyone loves to hear the story of the underdog who overcame obstacles and succeeded because it inspires us to become better as we recognize that we can also overcome. The difference between Vern and Clyde is their mindset. How they gather and interpret information leads them to react differently and get different results.

Mindset

The first part of instilling self-belief is to recognize and be aware of the programs that may be limiting it. The domesticated adult elephant is tied to a post and remains tied because it has given up. It is not aware of the tremendous power it has gained as an adult to break the rope or rip the post from the ground. It has stopped looking for fresh solutions to free itself at an early age and has no belief that it can.

Embrace Gratitude, Instill Self-Belief, and Seek Excellence

The memory of an elephant.

Circuses train elephants when
they are young. They bind one of
their legs to a post. The baby
elephant will fight and fight to
get free.

He eventually gives up.

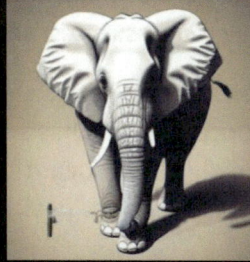

The adult elephant could get free but believes the internal lie
that he does not have what it takes to live free.

Later in the book, you will discover what it takes to break free of
limiting beliefs. The Innoptimax™ process will guide your
journey to continuously find new ways to higher levels of
achievement.

For now, let us explore the characteristics of the mind so that
we can use it for purposeful means.

The Conscious Mind

Sometimes, our greatest powers lie in differences that we may
perceive as weaknesses. We want to develop awareness of our
talents and powers before we can take possession and use
them effectively to reach our objectives. One of our greatest
powers as human beings is the power of choice. We can choose
different pathways, and in doing so, create and mold our future
in a specific direction.

This conscious mind is one of the primary tools to instill self-
belief as it is the seat of the will and may impress the
subconscious. It has the faculty of discrimination and has the
power of reasoning. Harmony within oneself creates a ripple

Embrace Gratitude, Instill Self-Belief, and Seek Excellence

effect of harmony in the outside world, leading to improved health, greater success, and the best of all outcomes.

The conscious mind is dichotomous in such that it thrives on comparisons. It also has a single focus. It does not multi-task but can rapidly switch focus from one task to another. Asking it to do so is not ideal for peak performance.

The mind also increases results when it is slowed down. It is important to recognize that your conscious mind follows your focus. Your focus is the boss, and the mind will filter events that do not support your thoughts and dismiss other activities outside of your focus.

Our single focus is a double-edged sword that must be recognized and acknowledged. It is recommended to take great care in choosing what we feed our mind as it continuously works to find reasons to justify actions and thoughts over time. Hence if you ask a question like "What is wrong with me?" It will look for evidence to answer it and can lead you to self-harm. If you ask better questions like "where do I excel?" It will work for you to show evidence of your capabilities and your value.

Beware of what you feed your conscious mind.

Finally, while you may forget certain things, there is no erase button.

The Subconscious Mind

The subconscious mind never sleeps, never rests, any more than does your heart, or your blood flowing through your veins. The subconscious mind is the seat of our principles and our aspirations.

The subconscious mind does not engage in the process of proving. It relies upon the conscious mind, "the watchman at the gate," to guard it from mistaken impressions. It holds our emotions and will always win over the conscious mind. It has been found that by plainly stating to the subconscious mind certain specific things to be accomplished, forces are set in motion that lead to the desired results. [11]

A Harvard study concluded that 95% of our purchase decision making takes place in the subconscious mind. [12] The business world has paid notice and leverages brand power as an attractive option for making product decisions. As an expert on strategic pricing for analytical instruments, I have observed that pricing is rarely the dominating factor in decision making. Brand recognition built on quality and service plays a key role. When faced with a choice the human brain is always looking for a way to take a shortcut to avoid deep, deliberate thinking.

While some may tell you that the television and the media have no influence on your children, they are at the same time charging companies millions of dollars for the opportunity to influence your buying habits. Individual companies invested up to $6.5M for thirty-second commercial ads during the 2022 Superbowl to influence your buying decisions. Either they are wasting money, or they know something about influencing people. You be the judge.

BEWARE!

Your subconscious mind is like a computer or machine and knows nothing except what it has been fed. [13] Leading behavioral researchers have told us that as much as seventy-

---

[11] Haanel, C. F. (2010). The Master Key system. SoHo Books.
[12] The Subconscious Mind of the Consumer (And How To Reach It). (2003, January 13). HBS Working Knowledge. https://hbswk.hbs.edu/item/the-subconscious-mind-of-the-consumer-and-how-to-reach-it
[13] Martin, F. (1995). Hung by the tongue. Francis P. Martin Pub.

seven percent of everything we think is negative, counterproductive, and works against us. Medical researchers have said that as much as seventy-five percent of all illnesses are self-induced. [14]

Our natural programming over the years has left us fearing for what could be – the unknown. Indeed, our decisions determine our future, and the outcome is never certain. Our subconscious brain suffers from what it has learned – pessimism – or the tendency to expect the worst.

Consequently, we want to reprogram our mind to build self-belief to a new sense of self-worth and self-esteem. Striving to repeatedly see the "good" in a situation will enable your subconscious mind to readily choose the positive side of a situation and naturally anchor its focus on a "Can do" attitude. You will become unstoppable.

The great news is that you can influence your subconscious mind regardless of your past experiences.

You can learn to make your subconscious work for you towards reaching your aspirations. Becoming aware of its power and understanding how to use it is the first step to greater accomplishments.

Changing the program
When they were younger, I instructed my children not to engage in conversation with strangers when we were not present. While this instruction may make sense to protect a six-year-old from getting kidnapped, it does not make sense for an

---

[14] Helmstetter, S. (2017). What to say when you talk to your self. Simon and Schuster.

adult. I mean, I weigh around 200lbs, am almost six feet tall and feel robust enough to fight off a kidnapper.

When was the last time that you reflected on reprogramming your brain to recognize that it is okay to talk to a stranger? Weren't each of our friends a stranger at some point?

If we desire to be successful and build a strong network of people, we must change our mental program to make new connections. We cannot set an expectation that a specific person will reciprocate our gesture; just like we cannot force someone to love us.

There is nothing to lose in saying "Hello."
You may make a friend.

If someone does not respond back or is negative, it is not a reflection on you but on them. With this perspective in mind, we are equipped to go out where there are people, to smile and say "hello" with the aspiration of a positive response.

It's an inside job

Contrary to usual thinking, self-belief is not from outside of us. It results from the confidence we build by accomplishing trivial things that accumulate as proof of our "ableness" to succeed in any endeavor. Small things lead to bigger things. With time, we create self-belief and realize that it is "an inside job."

No amount of outside encouragement or prodding will give us self-belief unless we **decide** to trust ourselves and "do as if" until our self-belief develops into a strong, powerful, and unstoppable feeling that we can overcome. Self-belief is the key to Peak Performance as It empowers us to do our best every time out. It is one of the most important virtues for achieving success.

Having faith in yourself and your abilities is essential for pushing through challenging times, tackling challenging tasks, and making the most of opportunities. Self-belief gives you the confidence to take risks, think creatively, and reach for the stars. It is the foundation of resilience and the key to unlocking your potential.

When you believe in yourself, you can focus on the present moment, take control of your life, and create the future you desire. With self-belief, anything is possible. Believe you can overcome obstacles, and you will.

> *"Believing in yourself is the first step to accomplishing any goal. If you think you're going to fail, you probably will."*
> **- Will Smith**

The internal battle

The biggest battles in the world are not external battles but internal battles. As you start to think bigger you may feel a force pulling you back down to your old habits. This is your subconscious mind reacting to a proposed change. Just like the

horse, it wants to go back to the original program to "protect" you from change.

> *"Everyone you meet is fighting a battle that you know nothing about. Be kind."*
> **- Robin Williams**

Your subconscious mind wants to stay the course and stick to your old mental programs. It wants to keep you tied to the post like the adult elephant where it feels secure. It wants to get

Embrace Gratitude, Instill Self-Belief, and Seek Excellence

back to a state of familiarity and comfort and will fight you for a brief period until the latest programs replace the old ones.

Research informs us that it takes about 20 to 30 days to create a new synapse in our brain. You can expect that it will take three to four weeks before a new brain pattern is created and that your subconscious brain accepts a new idea.

Have you ever asked yourself "Why is it that some people succeed using a proven formula while others do not? François Lupien, a professional sales coach, explains it as follows. "5% of success is strategy ("The Proven formula") and 95% is mindset. If you have a strategy that improves results by 10X you will get 10 x 5% = 50%. On the other hand, if you improve your mindset by 10X you will have an impact of 10X 95% = 950%.

Mindset is why we do not do what we know we should do. The mindset is why people feel stuck with small results while knowing they could do more. It is also why people who have nothing more than their self-belief feel they can reach for the moon and then proceed to build methods and tools to get there.

Your Know-Edge™

Whatever field of expertise you choose, you will find someone who has specific knowledge that is greater than yours. While this may feel intimidating, you should embrace their knowledge as they can provide insights that will guide you in your journey.

If we represent all the knowledge known to humankind as a large blue circle, we could then illustrate the general knowledge learned from kindergarten to high school as a smaller green circle in the middle.

Some people will study in a specific field and increase their knowledge and push the boundaries of human knowledge to expand the larger outer circle. Those people are called doctors.

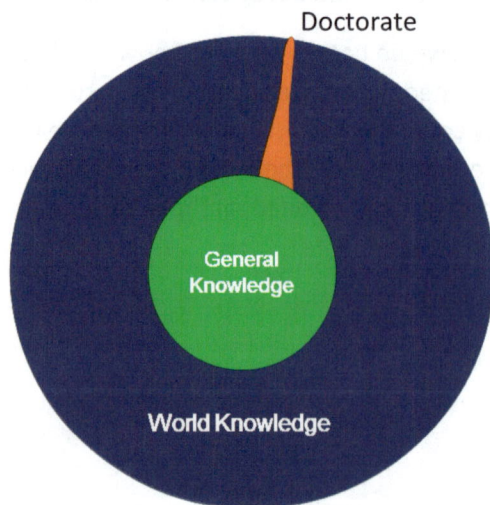

Each of us has our own special knowledge that is aligned with our interests and passion. This knowledge represents the area where we contribute to conversations as well as projects at work. These are the things you know that give you an edge, your Know-Edge™. You are responsible for it, and you can

Embrace Gratitude, Instill Self-Belief, and Seek Excellence

always expand it by reading and studying a topic that you are enthusiastic about. Investing your time strategically in building your Know-Edge™ increases your value.

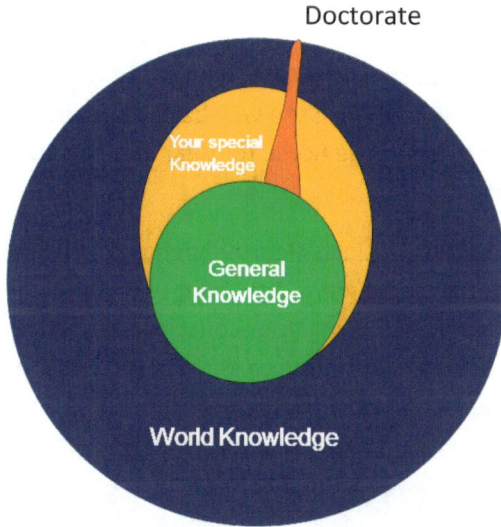

Doctorate

Your special Knowledge

General Knowledge

World Knowledge

Your Know-Edge™ can be helpful to the doctor by broadening the scope of their research. They can help increase the depth of your special knowledge to have greater influence in the future. Build your Know-Edge™ and reach out to experts in your field to learn from them and share your special knowledge. Believe in your capabilities and share them with the world.

Guiding the horse

Horses are notorious for going back to the barn when spooked. When I was younger, we lived next to a ranch where they provided horseback rides. They had a lead horse in the front and all the other horses followed.

My older brother and I went for a ride and passed in front of our house along the way. He convinced our group leader to

Embrace Gratitude, Instill Self-Belief, and Seek Excellence

grant him permission to cross the street and show his horse to my parents. Everything went well until the horse realized that he was no longer on the original trail and, more importantly, without a lead horse.

This horse went back to his habitual trail and ran (my brother would claim that it flew) all the way back to the barn with my brother holding on to the horse for dear life. Fortunately, no one got hurt.

Like the horse, our instincts (learned behaviors) will bring us back to our original program. You want to train your subconscious mind by using your conscious rational brain to guide your subconscious mind to learn new tricks. They eventually replace the old program with practice and repetition until your mind goes to the new trick by default.

Our subconscious mind is like a horse. It is strong and powerful, and difficult to control when under pressure.

Faith

My mentor, André Blanchard, used to say that people spend more time planning two weeks of vacation than they do planning their future. We make decisions every day based on faith. When we book a flight, we have faith that we will be healthy at the time of the flight. When we go to work, we have faith that we will be back at home safely in the evening.

Our faith gives us strength during challenging times in a way that enables us to keep going even when things seem impossible. With faith we trust that things will work out in the end. It gives us the courage to take risks and to believe in ourselves, a key to unlocking our potential and achieving our goals.

> *"We are not human beings having a spiritual experience.*
> *We are spiritual beings having a human experience."*
> **- Pierre Teilhard de Chardin**

Without faith, there is no reason to have self-belief in your capacity to influence your future. It takes faith and self-belief to make a space and set a time for yourself to reflect on what you desire and aspire to achieve.

Setting a space and time strategically to pause and ask yourself the right questions to achieve greater results adds worth that is greater than **any** other task. Work on honing your skills to the point where you believe that you are the best person to present your value proposition. **YOU are worth as much as anybody else,** and **your ideas** add unique perspectives that add value.

I recommend setting a time in your calendar to think and reflect on what you can improve, what you should continue to be doing, and what you should let go.

Embrace Gratitude, Instill Self-Belief, and Seek Excellence

If you approach life with gratitude, feel blessed, and have faith, why would you accept any suggestion that nourishes doubt or fear?

Fear and faith cannot co-exist together. If you have one, you do not have the other.

Develop good habits

As previously stated, it takes about 20 to 30 days to create new patterns in our brain. You have worked for years to condition your mind to where it is Today, and it has done an excellent job in following your directives and bringing you exactly where you wanted. Be patient as you learn new habits, the results will come soon enough.

It is claimed that Dr. Karyn Purvis, best-selling author, and world-renowned developmental psychologist, had found and stated that it takes approximately 400 repetitions to create a new synapse in the brain, unless it is done in play, in which case it only takes 10 to 20 repetitions. [15] While it will take some time and effort to change brain patterns, it is interesting how the process can be accelerated through play.

Remove sources of negative stimuli

What comes out of our mouth is a direct result of what we have allowed into our brain. Even if we have the capability to filter out information, our subconscious brain records everything that is passing through our eyes and ears. Therefore, our

---

[15] Helping Children Heal from Trauma: The Lessons of Dr. Karyn Purvis. (n.d.). CASA of Travis County. https://www.casatravis.org/helping_children_heal_from_traum a_the_lessons_of_dr_karyn_purvis.

environment can play a significant role in our perception of events.

Separating negative input from positive input requires effort and energy. While it is a worthwhile effort, it is better and more efficient to remove sources of negative input. Examine the channels that are feeding our old mental programs. In some cases, all that may be needed is to affirm yourself and inform people that your two ears are not garbage cans for people to dump their negative thoughts. Other times, you may need to sever ties from negative influences. Remember that a close friendship is defined by three things. It is lasting, positive and reciprocal. [16]

Speak of what you want

What do you say when you talk to yourself? What type of images and stories do you visualize? What habits have you developed when it comes to guiding your brain? Are the scenarios in your brain positive or negative? Are they constructive or destructive?

The brain's ability to focus can be a two-edged sword. On one hand, it can be a great asset, allowing us to concentrate on a task and achieve remarkable results. On the other hand, if we focus on negative things, it can be a hindrance, as it can lead to tunnel vision and cause us to miss key details or opportunities.

Focusing on negatives can also lead to stress and anxiety, as we become overwhelmed by the task at hand and unable to take a step back to look at the bigger picture.

---

[16] Denworth, L. (2019). Friendship: the playbook: How to Apply the Science of Friendship. W.W. Norton Inc.

Embrace Gratitude, Instill Self-Belief, and Seek Excellence

My father was a teacher in his early career. He taught me that if you told a class not to put gum under their desk you would find the underside of all desks covered with chewing gum by the end of the semester. On the other hand, students would throw gum in the garbage if your instruction were to throw used chewing gum in the garbage can (the behavior that you want).

 or

Communicating what we want and not what we do not want is a simple recipe that works very effectively.

When a child exhibits unruly behavior, it is important to address it. . . Seize moments of good behavior and acknowledge them promptly with encouragement to support the good behavior that we aspire from the child.

A simple statement reminding a child of past behavior such as "you know, when you did this . . . it made me happy and proud." or, "I really like it when you do this . . .", are effective reinforcement approaches that will go a long way in encouraging the behavior that you seek.

Consider the analogy from the book "Men are from Mars and Women are from Venus." [17] . Our brain is Martian. If you send your mind a message showing long blades of grass to remind yourself to cut the lawn you will, without a doubt, end up with the longest grass in the neighborhood.

Before my wife and I adopted our son, we learned an important lesson during one of the preparation courses. We were informed that parents who self-promote themselves stating how lucky their child is to have them as their adoptive parents will create feelings of inadequacy, unworthiness in the child.

The insight was that, as adoptive parents, we are asking for a child to complete our family and are the lucky ones when a match is found. I feel blessed with this experience to share love with our son. We continuously thank God for giving us such a kind and intelligent boy and for each of our wonderful children.

The same applies when leading an organization. Just because it is someone's job does not mean that we cannot recognize when a job is well done and acknowledge it.

Recognize when a task is well done and promote the behavior. Everyone appreciates a genuine compliment.

During a culture development program with a group of managers/leaders someone asked if leaders should focus on the positive people or the negative ones. In my mind it is simple, focus on the positive people and promote them publicly and address the negative people in private.

---

[17] Gray, J. (2004). Men Are from Mars, Women Are from Venus: The Classic Guide to Understanding the Opposite Sex. Harper Collins.

To increase attendance in meetings, I would send a follow up message to everyone to congratulate the attendees for their participation and highlight a few of the best discussion points. Those who were not present in the first meetings quickly saw the value from the discussion points and showed up at the next meeting.

Cut-and-splice

One of the challenges in replacing a limiting belief is to identify and recognize it in the first place. If everyone around you believes that the earth is flat, it may be difficult to recognize how this belief/program is limiting your capabilities to see the world.

When you are thinking "Inside the box" you have no evidence that there is anything to gain from thinking differently. In addition, fear of falling off the earth may dissuade you. This is a key area where the feedback of a good coach can make a real impact.

The cut-and-splice method is an effective method to replace an old program with a new one. Imagine the film of a movie, or audio tape recording, and wanting to remove an unwanted scene from it. You will take the unwanted section of the tape, cut it out, and replace it with a new scene.

The same technique can be useful to replace old mental programs with new ones in our mind.

"Stop" yourself from your thinking track when you become self-aware of negative self-talk. You can even say "Stop" vocally as an effective way to take a pause.

Remind yourself that this old program is no longer wanted. Choose words that describe the "new scenario" - the behavior and results that you want. Repeat these words aloud a few times to make an impression in your mind. Finally splice this new scenario so that it replaces the old section that you had just cut out.

A fantastic way to identify old programs that are stopping you from a breakthrough transformation is to observe and look for people who are living with your desired lifestyle; those who have already broken through to new paradigms.

My experience informs me that those who have left the old paradigm get joy in pulling others to join towards them into their collective group. In their book, "Tribal leadership," Dave Logan, John King & Halee Fischer Wright provide great insights on how people form natural groups and how you can recognize the groups ("Tribes") that seek to work together. [18]

> **An elderly man advised a friend of mine.**
>
> **"When the lead scout goes too far in front of the army, they can be mistaken for the enemy. "**

This is a reminder that as a leader, you will want to enable your team to follow you as closely as needed to ensure that they never feel left behind.

Use your creative imagination

The power of imagination can be used in many ways. It does not require more effort to create a positive image in our mind than a negative one, it is simply a question of habit.

A high percentage of the negative thoughts that have coursed through your mind have never materialized.

How often have you been lying to yourself with "what if" questions, negative scenarios, concerns that have never materialized. More importantly, how many times did you accept these lies like the adult elephant tied to a post?

Let us imagine a new scenario. You are working continuously on honing your skill which separates you from the norm. You are viewed as a prominent successful person who multiplies productivity times ten. You are recognized and perceived to be at the height of your profession and are only getting started in

---

[18] Logan, D., King, J., & Fischer-Wright, H. (2011). Tribal leadership: Leveraging Natural Groups to Build a Thriving Organization. HarperBusiness.

making an impact. People are cheering for you and thousands are applauding your accomplishment as you get recognized for your contributions to your community. Lives have changed positively because of you. You give generously to people in need and inspire people to a better life.

Take a minute to close your eyes and imagine the feelings flowing through you in this scenario. How would your day progress if you generated these feelings every morning purposefully?

This exercise may feel strange if you have never imagined yourself in this scenario before. You may feel like you are telling yourself a lie. If that is the case, let me ask you a question. Haven't you been lying to yourself with all the negative, unfounded, negative scenarios that you have let course through your brain?

What do you think will happen to the probability of reaching your goals if you visualize yourself reaching them for two minutes every day vs imagining barriers? There are enough challenges in life without adding imaginary ones into your mind. It is the most powerful tool that you own.

My priest once gave our congregation a challenge. He instructed one person in each couple to say, "God is good all the time." and for the other person to respond, "All the time, God is good." He challenged us to take notice of the transformation in our life once we had done this for 30 days.

My wife and I played along and noticed a state of peace and comfort. We have continued to play this game for over a decade and use this formula when facing a challenge. The results are immediate.

I challenge you to create new pathways in your mind to create new habits that will allow you to use your mental "chainsaw" and carve new positive mental stories and colorful imagery that enables you to see yourself attain your greatest successes. Take the time to feel the positive emotions flowing through you.

Think Bigger

Thinking big is a skill and a habit that is formed through repetition. It is just as easy to use and channel your energy to think big about possibilities as it is to use it to think small and focus on roadblocks.

People tend to gravitate toward thinking about potential roadblocks and do not invest enough time to think bigger to find solutions.

> **"I think it is possible for ordinary people
> to choose to be extraordinary."**
> - Elon Musk

As mentioned before, the mind goes to your focus. Challenge yourself to think bigger and use your creativity to find possibilities. Look for what can be achieved without restrictions, not just what is. The probability of being considered for the next big opportunity increases when you elevate your thinking to a higher level and seek to understand how things fit at that level. Dr. Schwarts recommends developing the big thinker's vocabulary with big, bright, cheerful words. [19]

> **Thinking big stretches our mind and challenges our belief.
> Like an elastic band, a stretched mind never goes back to the old
> state. Stretch your mind and think bigger.**
> - Roger Joanis

---

[19] Shwartz, D. (1987). Magic Of Thinking Big. Simon and Schuster

Embrace Gratitude, Instill Self-Belief, and Seek Excellence

This, in essence, is a breakthrough transformation.

Focus on your gifts

If I wrote on a board "A, B, C, F, G, H, J" and asked, "what is missing?" You would say "D, E and I." The problem is that you are trying to answer a poor question that is focusing on a gap. What if I told you that all that you needed to succeed is in fact "A, B, C, F, G, H, and J"? Then you would focus on these attributes without spending a second on "D, E and I" (no pun intended on DEI efforts).

This morning, I was helping my son on a school project focused on Hellen Keller. She was born Blind, Deaf, and Mute and learned to read and write in braille in the brief period of three years after being made aware of the power of communication through sign language.

Hellen Keller became an activist for the blind and wrote twelve published books in braille, an accomplishment that few people have achieved in their lifetime. She focused on the ability to communicate through the sense of touch instead of focusing on what some would consider to be a debilitating handicap.

Embrace Gratitude, Instill Self-Belief, and Seek Excellence

We are all born with some gifts that we are tasked to discover while on earth. My son asked me what his gifts were. I reminded him that he was intelligent, was great at telling stories and was in school to learn skills that would allow him to discover more of his gifts and share them with the world. Just like my son, we need to ask better questions.

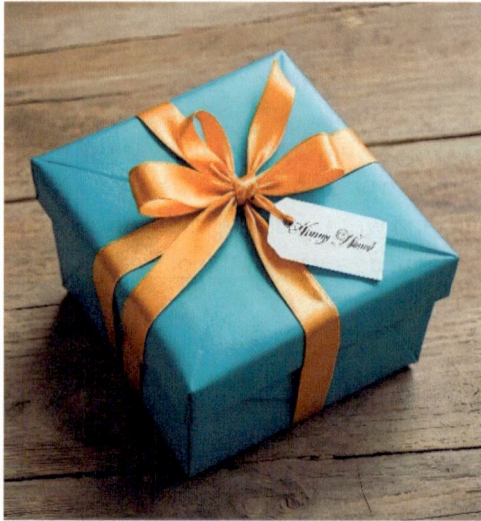

What are my gifts?

_____

_____

_____

_____

Action

Too often, we are stalled in our life journey because we fear facing unexpected barriers or challenges. We cannot predict the future and sometimes let fear overcome us because of past experiences or poor internal negative self-talk (our inner voice) which puts a disproportionate focus on negatives.

The walk to school.

A boy was avoiding a street on his daily walk to school because of his fear of being bitten by an angry barking dog.

One day, late for school and in a hurry, he took this shorter path only to have to face the dog and realize that it had no teeth.

 The reality is that most of the time, our fears have no bite, just like the toothless dog. All it takes is to reframe our thought process, remembering what we have already accomplished in the past, and we soon discover that "I can't do this" is just a knee-jerk reaction.

With a bit of insight, we may rediscover how we dealt with something similar in the past and found a way to overcome obstacles. It has to do with acknowledging our transferrable skills. Once we become conscious that we succeeded before, it is easier to say, "I can do this …."

Embrace Gratitude, Instill Self-Belief, and Seek Excellence

My father would reprimand us if he ever heard my brother, sisters, or myself state "I can't do it." He would respond that "I can't do it, doesn't exist" and would ask us to restate our position to something like "I can do . . . and I will do . . ."

The three little birds

"Three little birds are on a branch. Two of them are thinking of jumping off and see themselves flying above the forest.

How many birds are left on the branch?

-Roger Joanis

All three birds remain on the branch because they are only thinking of jumping and not actually jumping. This story taught me that t*hinking and doing are two different things.*

Action cures fear.
Indecision, postponement, on the other hand, fuel fear.[20]
- Dr. David J. Schwartz

So many reflections on how to instill self-belief! The fact is your self-belief meter will remain at the same level unless you decide to grow it.

As always, the choice is yours. You can go "steady on the course" or you can tighten your belt, plan to grow your self-belief and get on with the show. A lot will depend on your

---

[20] The Magic of Thinking Big, David J. Schwartz

Embrace Gratitude, Instill Self-Belief, and Seek Excellence

"WHY." Make sure you have a deep down "in your gut" reason to act.

We would like to suggest that since you have come this far, you owe it to yourself to drive toward a Breakthrough Transformation by applying simple actions to strengthen your self-belief.

Grit

Grit is a key attribute that many successful people possess. It is defined as a combination of passion and perseverance that enables individuals to stay focused and motivated towards achieving their goals, even when faced with difficult challenges or setbacks. It is an essential quality for success as it helps people to remain committed and resilient in the face of adversity. People who possess grit push forward and make progress despite the obstacles they may face.

Successful people understand that grit is a key factor in reaching their goals, and they make sure to cultivate it to stay motivated and focused on their goals. One way to cultivate grit is to think that the greater the struggle, the greater the reward.

The rain dancer

People claimed that a certain rain dancer could guarantee rain 100% of the time.

When asked about the secret of his success, he answered,

"Once I start to dance, I do not stop until it rains."

Embrace Gratitude, Instill Self-Belief, and Seek Excellence

I recommend any new salesperson to read "The go-getter" as an inspiring story about grit. [21]

> *Don't judge each day by the harvest you reap*
> *but by the seeds you plant.*
> - **Robert Louis Stevenson**

---

[21] Kyne, P. (2013). The Go-Getter: A Story That Tells You How to Be One.

Self-talk for building self-belief

Here are a few statements to provide examples of powerful affirmations that will empower you.

- I am special and unique. I love who I am, and I feel good about myself.
- I love how I feel, how I think, and how I do things.
- I am somebody with unique skills and ideas that contribute to making the world better.
- I am an excellent leader.
- I work consistently in a sustainable fashion and have a consistent approach to be an excellent leader.
- I nourish my body and mind in a way that makes me an excellent leader.
- I know how to approach situations and "always" choose to apply skills, concepts that help my team to be the best they can be.

Ideas to instill self-belief

1. List your Achievements: make a list of all your achievements, no matter how small. Look back on this list to focus on what you have already achieved. Become aware of your internal power.

2. Acknowledge your Know-Edge™: Take inventory of your transferrable skills: This list will provide insight on what you can achieve and overcome and expand the scope of what you can do. They are the basis for your internal power.

3. Sticky notes: Write short positive notes e.g., "I am a leader," on sticky notes and place them next to your mirror, next to your computer, on the dashboard of your car, . . . as reminders to use positive self-talk.

4. Mirror Work: Stand in front of a mirror and list out your positive traits and qualities. Look into your own eyes and talk to yourself as if you were talking to a friend.

5. Positive Affirmations: Read the "Affirm" section of this book to learn how to write positive affirmations to anchor into your subconscious mind.

6. Positive Self-Talk: Take a moment every day to talk to yourself using positive self-talk language.

Inventory of my Achievements

Things I Accomplished	Things I learned	Transferrable skills
_____	_____	_____
_____	_____	_____
_____	_____	_____
_____	_____	_____
_____	_____	_____
_____	_____	_____
_____	_____	_____
_____	_____	_____
_____	_____	_____
_____	_____	_____
_____	_____	_____
_____	_____	_____

Key take aways

- The conscious mind is the seat of the will and may be used to impress the subconscious.
- The subconscious mind is the seat of our principles and our aspirations. It holds our emotions and will always win over the conscious mind.
- Self-belief is an inside job.
    - Expect 20 to 30 days to change brain patterns.
    - Develop and own your Know-Edge™.
    - Guide and train your mind to focus on positivity.
    - Believe that you can.
- Remove negative influences.
- Speak of what you want.
- Cut negative impressions and splice them with positive ones.
- Reframe your self-talk using imagination with positivity.
- Build a habit of thinking bigger.
- Know that action cures fear.
    - Create an action plan.
    - Follow the plan without procrastinating.
- Remind yourself of your successes.

Never, never, never give up.

- Winston Churchill

Excellence

The third pillar of internal power is underpinned by a focused effort to seek excellence in all you do. We define Excellence as the discipline to do your best all the time, even when you do not feel like it.

When you set out every day to do your best, not be perfect, but be excellent in what you do, it does not matter if you feel good or bad. Doing your best means striving to put your best foot forward, having a cheerful outlook, being objective, helping others be their best, aiming to be perceived as a positive influence.

As with anything important to your personal advancement, there must be a reason to act. Searching and seeking excellence obeys the same laws of proportionality. If you want excellence, it will only happen if the effort is there to achieve excellence. You can be sure that it does not happen overnight.

Let's face it, excellence was likely never top of mind in your daily routine. Acquiring an excellence mindset must be deliberate and planned. Every day, when you wake up, it should be one of your daily goals. Otherwise, it's wishful thinking.

Like anything else, excellence is a learned habit that you acquire by doing a little every day to establish the mindset. It is uncanny how modelling excellence begets excellence. With time, you become a model for those around you. Then, they become your allies in producing the best possible outcomes.

Remember the expression "monkey see, monkey do." As a leader, seek excellence in everything you do. Then you will never have to ask for it. People will also automatically seek excellence.

Excellence is a decision and a quality or a state of being that corresponds to doing the right thing even when you do not feel like it. It is achieved through dedication, and a commitment to improvement and learning. It is a journey, an attitude, and a mindset. It is not a destination.

In sports, you may feel disappointment for not winning a game but will never feel guilty or have regret if you gave it your all, even when you did not feel at your best. The same applies to life. Are you giving it your all?

Excellence is the driving force behind success, allowing us to achieve our goals and reach our full potential. Excellence can help us to increase our confidence and self-esteem, inspiring us to strive for more. It can help us to develop our skills and abilities, enabling us to reach new levels of success.

Excellence can also help us to be more creative, pushing us to find innovative solutions to problems. Ultimately, striving for excellence can help us to lead a more fulfilling and rewarding life.

Seeking excellence is a lifelong task requiring motivation to keep at it every day with patience and persistence. The key to motivation is linked to finding a deep-down reason for taking action, your Why.

Embrace Gratitude, Instill Self-Belief, and Seek Excellence

Aiming for excellence

We must acknowledge that excellence is not a state of perfection but a quality decision to do the best that you can, do the right things and do them right. It is a decision that requires commitment.

On the other hand, perfection is a destination and the expectation of an ideal state of being that is impossible to achieve. Perfection is an unattainable goal that should not be confused with excellence. Aiming for perfection in every task is a sure recipe for failure that can affect your self-belief adversely. Instead, we recommend choosing to seek excellence over perfection.

It should not be a surprise that large market leaders like Danaher, Thermo Fisher Scientific, 3M, IBM, Procter & Gamble (P&G), Google, GE, Goldman Sacks, and others choose to invest in coaching to strengthen their leadership team.

They recognize the importance of coaching their leaders to enable and empower their teams to drive organizational success through effective and efficient involvement of people in a continuously changing environment.

The following table illustrates the impact of leadership training in a successful organization.

DBS Driving Leadership & Development

FOUNDATION FOR OUR CULTURE
- Structured leadership program
- DBSU training >1,000 associates annually
- >1,300 DBS certified practitioners globally

DBS TOOLS TO DRIVE RESULTS
- DBS Leadership Toolbox: *Best People Leader Expectations*
- Leadership Anchors
- D+I *Policy Deployment* initiative

~75% AVG. ANNUAL SENIOR LEADER INTERNAL FILL RATE SINCE 2018

Developing Leaders at Danaher

EXPERIENCE	COACHING	TRAINING
70%	20%	10%

Best People Leader Expectations

Building People & Teams **+** Building Organizations

EXAMPLES - DBS TOOLS:	EXAMPLES - DBS TOOLS:
Performance for Growth Cycle (P4G)	Leadership Anchors
Crucial Conversations	Policy Deployment
Change Management	Organization Assessment Cycle

Realizing the potential of our team

ᐯ DANAHER

Embrace Gratitude, Instill Self-Belief, and Seek Excellence

For the individual, excellence is about taking the time to ensure that you understand the task, that you have the necessary skills and knowledge to complete it, and that you are committed to getting it done to the best of your ability. You will take the time to think through the steps to do it in the most efficient way possible while producing the highest quality results.

A responsible leader will make sure that he or she has the necessary tools and resources to implement an impactful process by which the team or individual is enabled and empowered to get the job done. That takes reflection and a deep desire to foster growth in the team. It should be a dedicated focus to the best possible performance.

Aspire

What are your expectations for your future? Have you ever asked this question or thought of setting expectations? When we expect things, we are setting limits. A better question is "What are your aspirations? Aspirations release you from the limits of expectations.

Athletes who set expectations will typically slow down once the expectation is met. Employees who are asked to meet expectations will focus on meeting only what is expected.

It is reasonable to think that you may miss some goals and that you may not always get to your aspirations. But why set limitations mentally when you can release your creativity to aspire, inspire and achieve beyond your expectations. You may surprise yourself and exceed old expectations more often than you thought.

Raise the bar

My son began to pedal without training wheels at the age of seven. Talk about an experience of raising the bar. He was fearful that he would fall and would produce every excuse to avoid getting on the bike. When I removed the training wheels, within twenty minutes he was pedaling his bike and experiencing the joy of succeeding at a new task. Life is more fun when we are in the process of achieving and overcoming.

Developing the habit of raising the bar gets us to greater achievements. Create a habit of raising the bar and see where it leads you. Just like pedaling on a bike, if you fall, get back on and try again while focusing on the horizon.

> *Quitters never win.*
> *Winners never quit.*
> **- Vince Lombardi**

Define the "Where" to inspire the "Why"

Imagine waking up in the morning with excitement and going to bed at night looking forward to the next day.

> *And it's those who start with why, that have the ability to inspire those around them or find others who inspire them.*
> **- Simon Sinek**

When your actions, your "how" and your "what" are aligned with your "values" and your "why," you no longer see "work" in what you do and find joy in everyday activities. It does not matter what you do, and knowing how to do what you do, if you have not taken the time to find your "Why."

Embrace Gratitude, Instill Self-Belief, and Seek Excellence

Simon Sinek describes this process as the golden circle. [22] He explains and illustrates how those who are massively successful, either individuals or organizations, define their "Why" before the "How and the "What" so that all efforts are aligned. In an organization, this results with minds and emotions that, collectively, are directed to optimize efforts and minimize wastage.

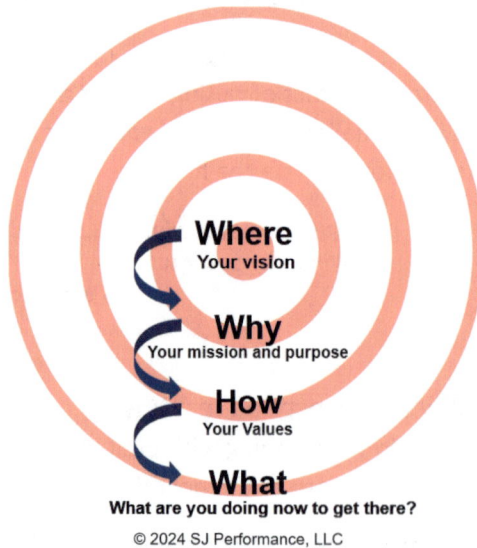

Where
Your vision

Why
Your mission and purpose

How
Your Values

What
What are you doing now to get there?

© 2024 SJ Performance, LLC

The question that logically follows is "how do you find your why?" The answer to this question is to first establish the "where." Your vision represents the "where." It is your vision, your dream, which inspires the "Why." To identify your "Why" you must first define where you want to go.

---

[22] Sinek, S. (2009). Start with Why: How Great Leaders Inspire Everyone to Take Action. http://ci.nii.ac.jp/ncid/BB07258461

Embrace Gratitude, Instill Self-Belief, and Seek Excellence

Find your reason for being

The Japanese word "Ikigai" means "reason for being." It represents your life's purpose; a space where four core elements of your life overlap. [23]

1. What do you love?
2. What does the world need?
3. What can you be paid for?
4. What are you good at?

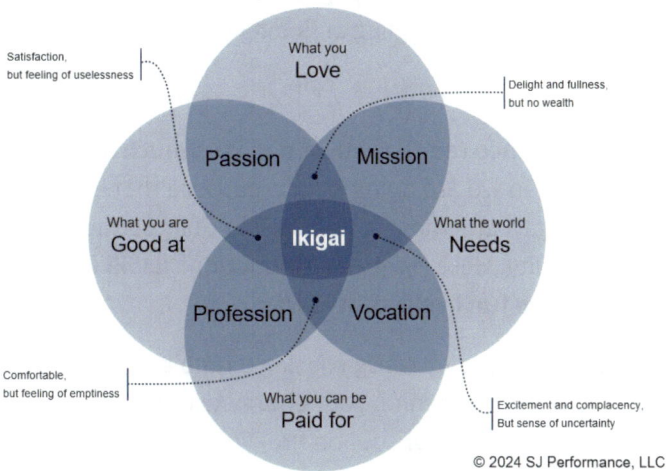

© 2024 SJ Performance, LLC

The intersect of these questions is where you will find your "reason for being" where you will feel most fulfilled.

Fundamentally, this image can serve to provide direction as a compass. After you have identified your current position, you can aim at the center and look at the opposite side of your current position to establish where you should focus to get closer to your Ikigai.

---

[23] García, H., & Miralles, F. (2017). Ikigai: The Japanese Secret to a Long and Happy Life. Penguin.

Embrace Gratitude, Instill Self-Belief, and Seek Excellence

Even google map asks at least two questions before you can reach any destination. The questions are:

1. Where is your current position?
2. Where do you want to go?

I recommend seizing this moment to pause and reflect on the four questions of the ikigai framework and evaluate where you are in comparison to your Ikigai. Again, **STOP** "just reading" and pause. These two preceding pages may be worth the entirety of the book if you are struggling in finding your purpose.

You cannot inspire people if you are not inspired yourself.

Seeking excellence requires effort and is so much more enjoyable when we are doing it for a purpose that is aligned with our "ikigai" and moving us closer to our goals to make our dreams a reality. Here is a great affirmation. **"I will find my Ikigai and have fun in the process."**

As the expression says, A dog chasing a rabbit is not bothered by fleas. When you channel your energy with focus on something that sets your soul on fire, your commitment to your goals becomes unwavering and you feel more fulfilled and happier. You take failure in stride as lessons that bring you closer to your goals and make you better.

Dare to live a life of purpose that is aligned with your "Why" and your values and share your passion with joy.

Find your Reason for being

1. What do you love?

_____

_____

_____

_____

2. What does the world need?

_____

_____

_____

_____

3. What can you be paid for?

_____

_____

_____

_____

4. What are you good at?

_____

_____

_____

_____

Key take aways

- Be the best of you.
- Do not aim for perfection.
- Think in terms of aspirations, not expectations.
- Find inspiration to inspire.
- Define your vision.
- Find your Reason for being.

Get Set. . .

We are now ready to go into each step of the Acreavis™ process to bring our mind and body in a ready state for peak performance™.

The process begins with activating our body and mind; oxygenating our blood to reach an optimal physical state of alertness and responsiveness to auto-suggestions.

We then work on relaxing and removing distractions by slowing down our brain for self-reflection and focus on specific thoughts.

We follow up with a strategy to nurture our mindset with affirmations formulated towards achieving our vision, mission, and values to internalize them and act congruently with them.

Finally, we provide a powerful visualization process to imprint our subconscious with our desired state of peak performance.

This method works to achieve personal goals with greater ease in business, sports, and life in general.

Activate, Relax, Affirm, and Visualize

Acreavis™

We use the term Acreavis™ to designate a process to:

1. Activate your mind and body in a systematic way to be mindful, intentional, and present.
2. Relax and slow down the brain to minimize distractions.
3. Affirm your desires and aspirations to create new mental pathways to Peak Performance™.
4. Visualize yourself, with emotions, as having reached your goals.

The order of these activities is also important as you will see.

We are again focusing on the internal power to produce the desired outcomes. We have explored the outside circle that emphasizes the mindset that underpins peak performance.

Activate, Relax, Affirm, and Visualize

The GrativatE™ process has set into place the foundational blocks towards having a mindset of excellence that underpins peak performance.

Once this is achieved, we progress to the inner circle with steps to enable the mind-body connection to work in unison to align all our forces (physical, mental, emotional, psychological, spiritual) to a single point of focus. This recipe follows the paradigm shift "from scattered to focused" as explained in *"AïM for Life Mastery™"*.

Acreavis™ brings to light the importance of training our five senses to a single objective, the way to maximize the impact of our effort both internally and externally. It also obeys the principle of "... DOING ONE THING AT A TIME, AND DOING IT WELL..."

Our objective is now focused on taping into the MIP™ to be mindful, intentional, and present. The Acreavis™ process allows us to increase our velocity in reaching peak performance™ with astonishing results when applied daily to address goals and objectives.

Before getting into each of the steps of Acreavis™ in detail, we will describe the MIP™ and go through a brief introduction of the AïM for life mastery™ process. to develop a heightened level of awareness of new paradigms, internalize them, integrate them into the routine, and master them.

Activate, Relax, Affirm, and Visualize

Conservation of energy

The first law of thermodynamics informs us that, in an isolated system, energy cannot be created or destroyed; it can only be converted from one form to another. The total internal energy of a system remains constant. It will only change through energy entering or leaving the system.

Translating this law to the process of achieving a higher level of performance allows us to deduct that we must manage our energy wisely. The objective is not to run continuously with the pedal to the metal, a recipe that inevitably results in getting burnt out. On the contrary, we want to slow down from time to time, in some areas, to accelerate and become more efficient going forward. Even race car drivers must slow down and negotiate curves on the road if they want to win, otherwise they'll end up in a ditch somewhere.

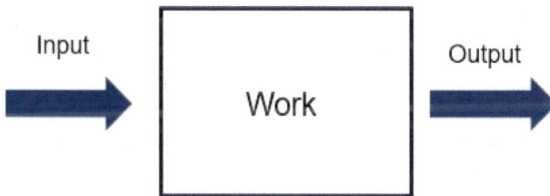

Input → **Work** → Output

It is important to recognize that nothing happens until we take action. Now, just any action will not do. It takes clear, defined, targeted action to produce a specific result.

Activate, Relax, Affirm, and Visualize

As human beings we have an ability to fill idle time with all types of activities to occupy our minds. Some of these activities could be replaced with intent to achieve a long-term vision towards a purpose. Case in point, the average person spends a total of 6 hours and 37 minutes looking at a screen each day, 2 hours, and 31 minutes on social media. [24] What would happen if we used one of those hours towards self-improvement? It would be the equivalent of working full-time on self-development for two months per year.

To quote Henry David Thoreau, "Most men lead lives of quiet desperation and go to the grave with the song still in them." [25]

Circle of Influence

The circle of influence offers helpful guidance on where and how to concentrate our attention when it comes to issues that we can manage. [26]

 The human mind can choose between being proactive or reactive to a stimulus. You can choose to react based on your feelings, which can be compared to a thermometer whose output is determined by the environment around it. We can never know what reading we will get from the thermometer until we face it.

No one can hurt you without your consent.
- Eleanor Roosevelt

---

[24] Moody, R., & Moody, R. (2023, March 15). Screen Time Statistics: Average Screen Time in US vs. the rest of the world. Comparitech. https://www.comparitech.com/tv-streaming/screen-time-statistics/
[25] Thoreau, H. D. (1854). Walden, Life in the woods.
[26] Covey, S. R., & Covey, S. (2020). The 7 Habits of Highly Effective People: 30th Anniversary Edition. Simon & Schuster.

Activate, Relax, Affirm, and Visualize

People who choose to be proactive make decisions based on principles and values which leads to consistency in their response. They can be compared to a thermostat that has influence on the environment around it.

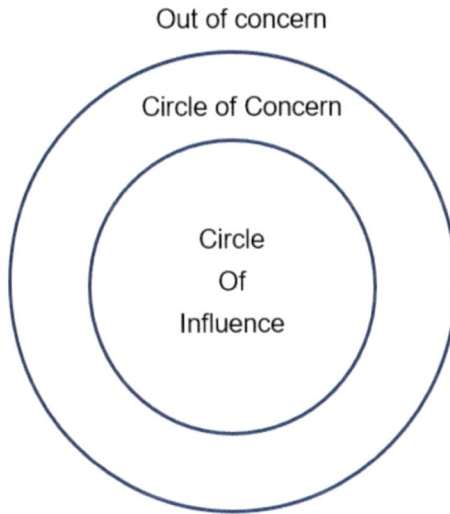

Out of concern

Circle of Concern

Circle
Of
Influence

Tapping into the MIP™

The second law of thermodynamics informs us that you can never make a machine that converts 100% of the energy. In the same way, our performance can always be improved to achieve better results with greater efficiencies.

Reaching Peak Performance™ involves using an approach that is structured, strategic, systematic and scalable to become more effective. We want to manage our activities and our energy in harmony with our purpose.

We would say that you are tapping into your MIP™ when you are **M**indful of the context, **I**ntentional on the purpose, and **P**resent. Achieving Peak performance™ is a decision that involves your MIP™ as you perform the following activities:

- Establish and focus on a compelling vision.
- Recognize and block sources of negative input.
- Overcome fears leading to self-sabotage.
- Develop a positive outlook towards your vision.
- Build and reinforce self-belief.
- Avoid distractions and waste.
- Make a strategic plan to use resources effectively.
- Follow your plan with excellence in mind.

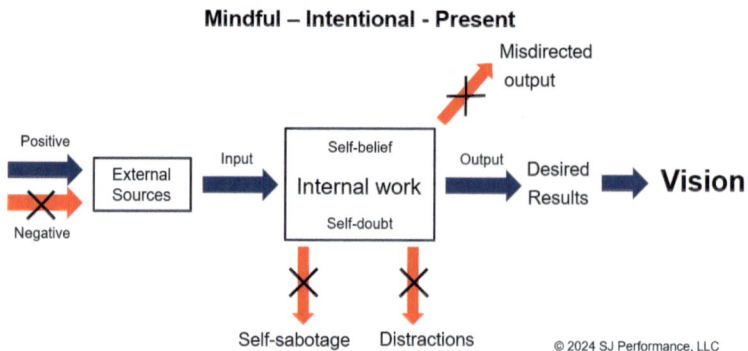

Mindful – Intentional - Present

Misdirected output

Positive

External Sources

Input

Self-belief

Internal work

Self-doubt

Output

Desired Results

Vision

Negative

Self-sabotage   Distractions

© 2024 SJ Performance, LLC

AïM for Life Mastery™

In his book, AïM for Life Mastery™, Raymond Perras provides a step-by-step process to empower you to reach your chosen level of performance while reducing stress. [27] He walks us through the steps of the journey: awareness, internalization, integration into the routine and mastery. As you will see, the AïM for Life Mastery™ process is a fantastic way to move you quickly along the tiers of competency.

Awareness

Do you remember making your first important purchasing decision: your first car, house, or bicycle. . .? Let us use a car as an example. You may recall that you did not pay much attention to cars prior to deciding that you wanted a car. Suddenly, shortly after you selected the model that you liked, you found cars of the same model all over the place. When you picked a color, you began noticing cars of the same model in the exact color that you wanted, and you would spot cars that may have been on your left or on your right and identified them.

What happened that made your car become so popular in your neighborhood so suddenly? What type of magic did you apply?

No magic at all. You expressed a desire that gave your brain an instruction, and then your brain did what it is designed to do. It focused on the goal, sorted through information to capture events that support your goal, ignored information that did not support your goal.

Imagine, If your brain had the power to help you achieve your long-term goals and objectives. Would you use this ability if it

---

[27] Perras, R. (2011). AïM for Life Mastery™: A Process That Will Empower You to Create Your Chosen Level of Performance While Reducing Stress.

Activate, Relax, Affirm, and Visualize

allowed you to recognize opportunities that you would not see otherwise? What would you use it for? Why? More importantly, would you be willing to do what it takes to learn how to use it effectively to reach your vision?

The good news is that you have this power as we just demonstrated. Once you are aware of this power you can instruct your mind to assist you to recognize opportunities that you may not have seen otherwise: a material object, a business solution, a key person that can help you achieve your next big goal.

Remember that your mind goes to your focus. It will alert you when you are close to your goal and are not expecting it. You do not have to strain your brain with intense focus to create awareness, on the contrary, it happens quite naturally once you identify a desire for something. When you slow down your brain to remove the constant inner chatter, you enable it to work for you to focus on what you want.

Let us go back to our first example. If your brain helped you with the purchase of your first car. What was your state of mind at the time? Was your mind racing everywhere or focused on a particular goal?

I will dare to say that your mind was calm, relaxed, and focused on the goal. That is because this is the state when our brain works best. Now that you are keenly aware of your inner power, you will want to create a strategy that is structured, strategic and systematic to create the right environment for your brain to thrive and accomplish this function in an optimal way.

Awareness begins with having a desire for something. We choose to be aware of certain things and choose to not pay attention to other things. If you want to take a test, look at the white Mercedes below. Go to a dealership and sit in one of them. Then take notice of how many white Mercedes are on the

Activate, Relax, Affirm, and Visualize

street in your neighborhood. You may be surprised at how good your brain is at finding them.

Do you remember your happiest moments in life? We are happiest when we are in the process of achieving. A newly married couple, with nothing but dreams in front of them, find happiness in the process of creating a family with harmony in the house.

I recall moving my family from Canada to the United States. I lived 7 months in a studio apartment of approximately two hundred square feet to prepare the way for my family as our daughter learned to speak English at school in Canada. My wife and daughter joined me in this apartment during the last 6 weeks. I recollect this as a fun experience that we compared to family camping as we anticipated to move to the new apartment that I had found. The immediate location was not important as we focused on the goal with a keen awareness of new opportunities.

Activate, Relax, Affirm, and Visualize

Personal Awareness

Personal awareness involves understanding one's own strengths and weaknesses, as well as recognizing the impact of one's own thoughts, feelings, and behaviors on others. It is an important part of emotional intelligence.

Increasing our personal awareness, with the right questions, allows us to identify areas of improvement and develop strategies to make positive changes and address any underlying issues that may be preventing us from achieving our goals.

The first step to reaching excellence is to become aware of our immense potential. Without this awareness people simply continue along the path of least resistance and remain content with the status quo. It is when our spirit is awakened through personal awareness that we become enabled and capable of achieving what was once considered impossible.

> *Success can lead to complacency,*
> *and complacency is the greatest enemy of success.*
> **- Brian Tracy**

As per Joseph Andrew, an American politician, the hardest decision in life is not between good and bad or right and wrong, but between two goods or two rights. For example, trading a good life for a great life.

Unconscious pessimism is a form of cognitive bias that prevents people from recognizing their own abilities and potential. It is a subconscious belief that one is not capable of achieving success or reaching one's goals. This type of pessimism can cause a person to doubt their abilities and make them less likely to take risks and try new things. They may become discouraged and feel like they will never be able to learn the new skill or reach the level of competence they desire.

Unconscious pessimism is often experienced when transitioning from unconscious to conscious incompetence as you challenge the status quo to grow. It is important to manage unconscious pessimism by recognizing it and developing positive self-talk that keeps your mind on your focus for continuous progress.

There is an expression that says, "You can't change what you do not know." While this is true, people can also choose not to know. There is plenty of evidence that suggests that the earth is round. Yet, there are still many who continue to believe that it is flat. They simply choose to read materials that support their belief and to ignore materials that do not. The mind is like a parachute; it works better when it is opened.

As you become aware of your capabilities, you will inevitably identify opportunities for growth. Identifying these opportunities is a necessary part of the strategic journey to a higher performance as it brings to the conscious mind new development areas that allow us to set goals and continue to grow. If you have not found any growth opportunities, then you are not thinking big enough or you are choosing to ignore the opportunities.

Activate, Relax, Affirm, and Visualize

Paradigms

The brain is a formidable tool that can do incredible things. Like any tool it can be used with or without a specific purpose. It can end up hurting you when misused. We, the human species, differ from other animals in how we create tools and use them to accelerate processes to reach our goals.

Paradigms are often the reason people get stuck and fail to progress. A paradigm shift occurs when new evidence or ideas not only challenge but also explain what cannot be explained through existing theories and beliefs. A shift to a new paradigm leads to a breakthrough transformation.

A Breakthrough transformation is one where you cannot go back to your old ways.

Because of their paradigm, the Swiss watch industry missed an opportunity to capitalize on a disrupting technology, the digital watch. The digital watch took over the market as the Swiss focused on their paradigm that a time recording instrument requires a mechanical approach with hands to tell the hour, minutes, and seconds.

One of the reasons why coaching is so effective in accelerating one's growth journey is that it introduces an outside perspective that can not only point out at growth limiting paradigms but also present and explain a new paradigm that will allow you to progress more quickly. A good coach can see the forest from the trees. They are a sounding board with a confidentiality agreement who can serve to validate ideas in a safe environment.

Activate, Relax, Affirm, and Visualize

Paradigm shifts

I recently visited the Yucatec-Maya archeological site of Ek Balam in Mexico and found it fascinating how Mayans were able to calculate the position of planets and understood how the earth took just over 365 days to go around the sun.

In contrast, on a different continent, the idea of a flat earth generated fear that kept sailors away from great expeditions. Proposing a new paradigm would be met with great resistance with people being burned at a stake for daring to challenge the views of the majority.

The lumberjack

A lumberjack returned his first chainsaw because it didn't work as well as his axe.

The chainsaw was beaten up and, curious, the storekeeper pulled the rope to start it and verify what was wrong with it.

The chainsaw started on the first stroke with a loud roar and the lumberjack jumped with a scream of horror "What's that sound?"

My father told me this story about the lumberjack who went through a change in basic assumptions (a paradigm shift) as he heard the motor for the first time to finally understand that you do not need to swing a chainsaw like an axe.

Activate, Relax, Affirm, and Visualize

The same can be said of our brain. When you begin to realize its capabilities, you immediately notice how people around you are not using it to its full potential. Progressing through a breakthrough transformation implies going through a paradigm shift, or many paradigms shifts that will free you from the shackles that prevent you from truly excelling and unleashing your inner powers.

To achieve a Breakthrough Transformation, we must be willing to change how we think. In his book, *AïM for Life Mastery™*, Coach P lists seven paradigm shifts that are most important and critical in shifting our thinking to enable personal

transformation to a better life:

1. Rigid to Flexible
2. Necessity to Possibility
3. Judging to Evaluating
4. Scattered to Focus
5. Blaming to Helping
6. Complaining to Problem-solving
7. Liking to Loving

I am going to guess that you have already gone through the first paradigm shift. Picking this book is a guarantee that you have opened your mind with the flexibility that is necessary to learn new ways to help you reach your goals.

The move from necessity to possibility can seem subtle. As you read on you will notice how people around you are caught in the paradigm of necessity. They are easily recognized as they use the words "I need" in their conversation. "I need this," "We need to do that." Crossing over to the paradigm of possibilities will result in language that sounds like: "I want this," "We aspire to do that," . . .

Activate, Relax, Affirm, and Visualize

There is an expression that states that "Beggars are poor." The use of necessity language over possibility language can be the difference between achieving a successful meeting and closing a new opportunity or missing out because the client subconsciously "feels" that you "need" them instead of having the desire ("wanting") to collaborate with them.

Needs language results in people sounding like beggars who lack something in their life. In contrast, people who think and speak in terms of possibilities attract more abundance in their life. These are the people who seem "lucky," but luck is simply an opportunity that is met with preparation. Lucky people have often prepared themselves mentally to recognize, welcome and accept the opportunity.

Recognize the failure diseases.
Let us talk about the three common failure diseases: detailitis, excusitis, and procrastination. [28]

Detailitis is the tendency to become overly focused on the details of a task or project, causing the individual to become overwhelmed and unable to complete the task. It is a situation that we usually qualify as "paralysis by analysis."

Detailitis can lead to excusitis with people stating something sounding like "I will get started when I have all of the details." Excusitis is the tendency to make excuses for why something cannot be done or why it is not worth doing, again preventing the individual from starting.

The final failure disease, procrastination, is the tendency to put off tasks or projects, leading to missed deadlines and incomplete work. All three of these failure diseases can be

---

[28] The Magic of Thinking Big, David J. Schwartz

Activate, Relax, Affirm, and Visualize

detrimental to an individual's success, and it is important to be aware of them to achieve one's goals.

Remember, everything repeated over and over becomes a habit. Just like you can create good habits, harboring the diseases of detailitis, excusitis and procrastination result in habits that stop you dead in your tracks!

The introduction of computers and recent technological advancements of the last decades have led to an increase in another disease called "Urgentitis". It has taken a hold in many organizations and has led many to confuse activity and accomplishment. Racing in all directions without aim will not get you to your destination faster. Life is more of a marathon than a race and these diseases prevent many from reaching their potential.

The power of choices

Here is a statement that may challenge one of your paradigms if you are in a difficult position and feeling stuck. I understand that if you have been through something traumatic or are in a tough situation, you may want to reject the following statement. I ask that you read this chapter to the end to understand the good news behind the statement.

> *Accept that you are where you are and what you are because of your own choices and decisions.*
> **- Brian Tracy**

If you are upset and offended by this statement, you are now presented with a choice:

1. To reject the statement and throw this book away.
2. To keep on reading and seek to understand.

Activate, Relax, Affirm, and Visualize

This statement is not meant to state that everything that happens to us is under our control. We have plenty of evidence that dreadful things have happened in this world for thousands of years and that terrible things will continue to happen in the future.

The statement is meant to empower you. The good news behind it is that you have the power to decide to be in a better place tomorrow or to remain where you are.

> **All the flowers of all the tomorrows**
> **are in the seed of today.**
>
> **- Chinese proverb**

You are the architect of your future. You have the power to forgive and learn from difficulties or to hold a grudge and wallow in self-pity. Until you accept this responsibility for yourself, you will be stuck and unempowered to improve your life as you are placing your future in someone else's hands.

I aspire for this book to bring some thought-provoking concepts that will challenge existing limiting beliefs. You may be surprised and react strongly like our lumberjack and his new chainsaw. If that is the case, you are encouraged to do your own research to gain a deeper understanding of this topic. You are also encouraged to follow the sequence of this book to apply the principles in an effective way.

Internalization

Internalizing new processes helps to ensure that the skills and knowledge learned are embedded in our long-term memory. This enables us to use the learned information and skills in a variety of situations and contexts. It also helps promote the development of transferable skills, which can be used in different contexts and situations.

Activate, Relax, Affirm, and Visualize

Internalization is important because it allows us to apply and adapt the skills we have learned to new tasks and challenges. Furthermore, internalizing new processes encourages the development of critical and creative thinking skills, which are essential for success in any field.

Successful salespeople have learned to ask questions that allow their clients to internalize the implication of not choosing their product and maintaining status quo. In a comparable way, how important is it that you overcome your challenges as a leader? How would you feel if, five years from now, you did not progress and found that your mindset and your choices were the only things holding you back? What is the implication of maintaining the status quo in your personal life?

I am hoping that these questions will help you to renew your mindset and identify personal goals that are important to **"YOU."**

Integration into routine

In business, integrating new processes into the routine can be a difficult and time-consuming process. A good first step is to document the current routine and map out how the new processes will fit into it. This helps to identify any potential problems or conflicts that may arise. Once the new processes are integrated, it is important to monitor the results to make sure that the new processes are working as intended.

Communication is key throughout the entire process. You want to keep all stakeholders informed of any changes or issues that may arise. With the right planning, integrating new processes into the routine can be a successful and rewarding experience.

At a personal level, once we have consciously internalized a new concept, we want to integrate it into our routine. There is a

Activate, Relax, Affirm, and Visualize

saying that practice makes perfect. André Blanchard taught me that this is incorrect; practice makes permanence. If you practice the wrong stuff long enough it will become a habit that is engrained in the routine.

It is like pressing on a key at the wrong time when playing a song on a musical instrument. The more you practice, the less you notice the wrong key stroke. The song is still good but not excellent. It often takes another person, a music teacher, to point out the differences.

Find your "Why" and then schedule a regular time to work on your vision and repeat it frequently so that it becomes a habit. Make it a priority to invest time in practicing applying the right stuff towards building your future. You will enjoy the process of pursuing your dreams.

Mastery

Mastery is the state of Effort-*Less* Effectiveness™ where one has reached unconscious competence. The body is aligned with the subconscious mind and both align with the conscious mind to produce best results. It is at this point that a person applies the right stuff, in the right amount, at the right time, towards excellence.

The key to mastery is practicing doing the right stuff, in the right amount, at the right time to create permanence in a relaxed state and in a state of performance.

Some people will get to mastery quicker than others because they do not need to undo years of unhealthy habits before applying the good habits. The longer you proceed with a bad habit and the longer it will take to adjust. Consider coaching as an opportunity to receive feedback to apply corrections before bad habits become engrained into the routine.

Activate, Relax, Affirm, and Visualize

Reflection time.

Where can I influence a positive change in myself?

_____

_____

What can I do now to improve results by 10% while recognizing that I am enough?

_____

_____

What is holding me back?

_____

_____

What will I do this week and next week that will help me progress to become who I want to be?

_____

_____

Take a pause to reflect on how you will feel when you accomplish your goals, visualize yourself having reached them. Remember this feeling and anchor it in your mind.

Activate, Relax, Affirm, and Visualize

Activate

Activation is based on the idea that action is the key to achieving success. As powerful as our brain is, we cannot simply think ourselves into success without following up with action. The best way to do this is to focus on the present moment and do something in that moment.

The concept of activation encourages you to act now, rather than waiting for the perfect time or opportunity to come along. By activating in the present moment, individuals can create positive change and move towards their goals.

Carl Rogers was an American psychologist and one of the founding fathers of the humanistic approach to psychology. He emphasized the importance of empathy and unconditional positive regard in helping people reach their full potential. He emphasized the importance of self-actualization and encouraged people to take responsibility for their own lives. Rogers believed that each person has the capacity to reach their goals and that a supportive, non-judgmental environment is necessary for growth.

While self-actualization is a good concept, it needs to be accompanied by action.

Activate, Relax, Affirm, and Visualize

One great example of activation is the Haka, a dance about the celebration of life performed by the Māori people in New Zealand. One type of Haka was made famous around the world by the All Blacks rugby team, and more recently, the haka performed by 21 year-old Hana-Rawhiti Maipi-Clarke, New Zealand's youngest MP since 1853, in her first speech in parliament..[29]

Activating the body

As the saying goes, "Mens sana in corpore sano" is translated to " A healthy mind in a healthy body". To activate our brain, we must first activate our body, get blood flowing.

As per Gavin Bradley, Director of Active working, "Metabolism slows down by 90% after 30 minutes of sitting. The enzymes that move the bad fat from your arteries to your muscles, where it can get burned off, slow down. The muscles in your lower body are turned off. And after two hours, good cholesterol drops 20%. Just getting up for five minutes is going to get things going again. These things are so simple they're almost stupid... "[30]

The idea of activating the body is to get blood flowing so that you get more oxygen into your brain. It may seem basic, but we spend most of our days with our arms down. Simply raising your arms above your head is a way to wake up the body.

Any exercise can work. A method that is effective and efficient is a breathing exercise coupled with arm movements. Moving your arms up and down as if lifting a weight, several times while

---

[29] Te Ao News. (2023, December 12). Hana-Rawhiti Maipi-Clarke delivers maiden speech [Video]. YouTube. https://www.youtube.com/watch?v=7ZOIlk9A6-8
[30] Ryan. (2023, July 12). Sitting is the New Smoking - The Risks of Extended Sitting. Start Standing. https://www.startstanding.org/sitting-new-smoking/

breathing IN and OUT with each pump, will increase your heart rate while promoting oxygen intake.

Find a set of short exercises that require moving your arms: e.g., run on the spot with feet planted, only moving your arms (30 seconds as fast as you can). Or do throng twisters, planting feet apart, and moving from waist up left then right, then left... for 20 seconds. Another good one is doing the bird fly – arms bent at elbows and extended out, do the flapping motion (30 seconds as fast as you can). Guaranteed to work up a sweat!!!

Activate, Relax, Affirm, and Visualize

The increased pulse and speed of breathing will also raise your body temperature and bring blood to your brain. Repeat the movement up and down thirty times per repetition. Running that activation exercise three times with one minute rest in between is all you need to be fully activated and ready to address Step 2 – relaxation.

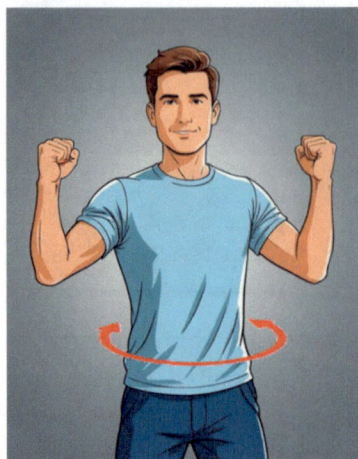

Voilà! You now have a method to activate physically in a way that is easy to understand, easy to apply, and easy to measure.

Relax

When we think of mastery of the physical body, we usually tie it to some form of rigorous movement and exercise. On the other hand, when we think of people having mastery of the mind such as Nelson Mandela, Mahatma Gandhi, the Dalai Lama, . . ., we picture a person that is more serene and at peace.

The optimal condition for our brain to perform is when it is slowed down and in a relaxed state. This allows the brain to block out distractions and use our mental energy to stay on task and achieve our desired outcome. Focus is particularly important when working on complex projects or tasks that require a great deal of concentration and effort.

The mindset

A mindset is a set of attitudes, beliefs, and habits that shape how you think, feel, and behave in different situations. It is a way of looking at the world and your place in it. We each have our own filters as we create a mindset that is positive or negative. Mindset can be influenced by your environment, experiences, and relationships. It is most strongly influenced by your "Why" as your mind goes to your focus looking for evidence to support your mindset and ignoring that which does not.

Activate, Relax, Affirm, and Visualize

Developing a stronger mindset can help you become more resilient and better equipped to manage the challenges that life throws your way. Ultimately, having a positive mindset is essential for successful living as it helps you stay focused on your goals and push through any obstacles that may come your way.

Meditation

Meditation is simple but does not necessarily come easily. Many people will resist it at first because of the effort required to get rid of disrupting thoughts generated by our brain.

> I meditated for the first time in a group session at the University of Ottawa. We were simply asked to observe the flame of a candle for about 30 minutes. The experience felt different, and I left the experience with a feeling of puzzlement. There was no moment of great revelation. . . I questioned if I did it right.

Do not worry about doing it "right." Even if you only slowed your mind for a few seconds during your first attempts, it is a success. With time, you will learn to slow down your brain activity for longer periods of time and feel more rested with greater focus.

There are many methods that you can choose from and perform from anywhere. Their goal is to calm the mind, observe our thoughts and emotions. With practice one becomes more aware of their own thoughts and can learn to focus on one thought to achieve inner peace and visualize higher performance.

Activate, Relax, Affirm, and Visualize

Neuro linguistic programming

Neuro-Linguistic Programming (NLP) was developed in the 1970s by Richard Bandler and John Grinder and focuses on the connection between the mind and language. [31] It is based on the idea that the way we think and communicate affects our behavior, and that we can use language to create positive change in our lives.

Let us examine the action of smiling as an example. It is believed that there is a close link between a physical smile and the mental state of joy and happiness. As a newborn, we observed people smiling and received instant gratification when responding with the same gesture. Our smile is deeply rooted as a program in our brain.

---

[31] Wikipedia contributors. (2024, February 24). Neuro-linguistic programming. Wikipedia. https://en.wikipedia.org/wiki/Neuro-linguistic_programming

Activate, Relax, Affirm, and Visualize

Neurolinguistic programming suggests that you can create the feeling of happiness by forcing yourself to smile. Forcing a grin up to your ears will result in experiencing joy and happiness.

In the same way, you can tie your relaxed state to a simple physical movement to function as a trigger (e.g., touching your index and thumb together while your hands are facing up during your relaxation breathing sessions). If you do this consistently and enough times you will be able to generate a state of relaxation at will during times of stress and high performance by simply putting your fingers together and going to a single, I-H-E cycle). We recommend bringing your thumb and index together as it is a small gesture that can be done inconspicuously with no one noticing.

Teaching your subconscious brain to respond to the NLP technique requires repetition and according to various research, it takes 20 to 30 days to install a new mental model (paradigm, brain circuits, axons and dendrites, circuit modification). That means sustained structured and continuous repetition.

A powerful way to accomplish that transformation is to have a daily program (preferably when waking up, and before going to bed) where you practice the breathing exercise religiously for 5-7 minutes.

Connecting mind and body

As you activate your body and mind, you will create a new habit and an opportunity to connect both together towards achieving peak performance™. It is the perfect time and place to reflect on things that you are grateful for and remind yourself of who you aspire to be.

Connecting mind and body for peak performance™

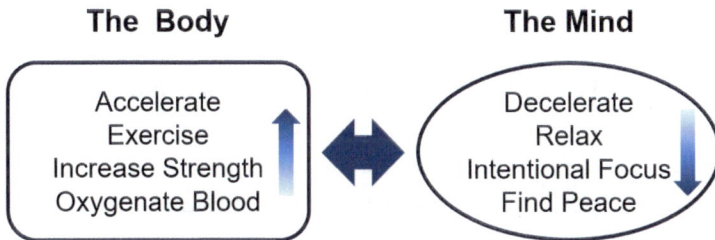

The Body	The Mind
Accelerate Exercise Increase Strength Oxygenate Blood	Decelerate Relax Intentional Focus Find Peace

© 2024 SJ Performance, LLC

We propose to perform the following activation method prior to delving into affirmations. Once activating the body and mind, you will be in the optimal environment to tap into your MIP™ so that you can maximize the impact of the affirmation and visualization processes within Acreavis™ to achieve peak performance™.

Activate, Relax, Affirm, and Visualize

Relaxing as a process

While relaxation techniques can be done from anywhere, we want to program this technique in our brain in a way that is structured, strategic, and systematic towards maximum Impact and mastery.

We present the 1-4-2 (I-H-E) method as a technique to anchor relaxation into our routine to have maximum effectiveness.

Here are the steps:

1. Practice in an environment that is quiet, comfortable, and with minimal distractions.
    a. While you may want to add soothing music, we do not recommend it as it could become a crutch and may not be available in moments of high performance when you need to relax.

2. Sit on a chair with your spine straight, your shoulders back and relaxed and your hands facing up while resting on your lap. 3R Posture©. [32]
    a. Rest
    b. Relax
    c. Recharge

---

[32] Perras, R. (2011). AïM for Life Mastery™: A Process That Will Empower You to Create Your Chosen Level of Performance While Reducing Stress.

Activate, Relax, Affirm, and Visualize

3. 1-4-2 Inhale, Hold, Exhale (IHE) programmed breathing.
    a. Inhale through your nose (1 count)
        i. Expand your abdomen (ensure only your abdomen moves and your upper chest stays immobile.)
        ii. Imagine diamond-like sparkles in the air and follow them entering your body.
    b. Hold (4 counts)
    c. Exhale through your mouth (2 counts)
        i. Exhale from your mouth, pursing your lips gently to create resistance to the air flow as it leaves your body.
        ii. Imagine grey specs also leaving your body. (You are purifying your body).

Take time to establish a process in a way that is structured, strategic and systematic to allow you to repeat an efficient and effective practice. With repetition, you are installing a new mental program where you can get to a relaxed state that you have linked to a breathing exercise.

It is important to use the same sitting position and breathing process during every practice in your mental gym to anchor the habit of relaxation in your mind and body as a basis to successfully achieve a complete cycle of the Acreavis™ performance framework.

SPICE™

During the development of our leadership think-tank, we developed an acronym to help anchor our grounding process in our mind and apply it at will at any moment of the day. When the mind is getting bombarded with different thoughts.

S = Sit

P = Palms up

I = Inhale   (1 count)

C = Calm the mind (while holding your breath 4 counts)

E = Exhale (2 counts)

We simply call for a Spice™ moment, adjust how we sit, and perform four consecutive breathing cycles. The results are consistent; a calm mind ready to engage in the next topic with renewed energy.

Affirm

We have activated our body and our mind to be alert physically and mentally. We have slowed down our brain which is now in the optimal state to receive new commands. Like a computer, your brain is subject to the GIGO principle (Garbage in, garbage out). You need to utilize the right syntax rules if you want the commands to provide the right results.

We know very well how to do affirmations because we are continuously talking to ourselves with our little voice. Affirmations are a form of self-talk; the trick now is to do it with awareness of the desired impact – new way of thinking – in a way that causes our subconscious brain to work as a PULL toward a successful achievement.

Affirmations should be expressed in action terms and supported with emotion and feelings to increase the impact on the subconscious brain.

One thing that is inescapable is the fact that we can only control changes within ourselves. So, any attempt at installing an affirmation that is directed at someone else will not be effective.

Activate, Relax, Affirm, and Visualize

Our subconscious brain only understands the action. It does not recognize the word no. If I say, "Don't think of Abraham Lincoln." You can already imagine his profile with his beard, and tall black hat. Abraham Lincoln is now in your mind because of me. Your subconscious mind will ignore negation and understand the action (e.g., "I don't smoke" is understood as "I smoke."

Characteristics of Affirmations

Let us look at the characteristics of effective affirmations. They need to be Positive, Present and Personal. It is not simply a matter of reading them but a matter of imprinting them in your brain with emotions.

Positive

The formulation must be performed using an affirmation sentence structure without any negative words or negation. The focus is on the goal and not the unwanted behavior. For example, you would not say "I will not drop the ball" Instead you would say "I catch the ball." I once walked on fire coals and was taught to think of the green grass on the other side of the hot coals. I understood that focusing on the hot coal was a sure way to get burnt.

The same logic applies if you were skiing in the mountains. You want to focus on the open space between the trees. If you look at the trees, you will find yourself aiming at them.

Activate, Relax, Affirm, and Visualize

Present

The present tense is an important consideration when making affirmations because it helps to create a sense of immediacy and urgency in the statement. By using the present tense, we can emphasize the importance of the affirmation and the importance of acting on it right now. As you progress in repeating the affirmation, you begin to build a sense of conviction that the words you are speaking are in the process of materializing. This encourages us to act to make the affirmation a reality.

At the beginning you may find yourself facing an internal conflict as you are stating a future state in the present and may not believe in the future state yet. The imposter syndrome, as it is known, is the experience of feeling like a fake or phony despite any genuine success that you have achieved. It is common to feel this way at the beginning and I would urge you to continue to press on and let your self-belief and skills catch up to your words.

Activate, Relax, Affirm, and Visualize

The subconscious brain does not know the difference between:

1) what is imagined, and what is real,
2) the past and the future, it only understands the present
3) the negative and the positive, only the action stated.

Personal

Your affirmations must be personal. They should be about you and only you. Attaching emotion to your affirmations will make them more effective as emotion will help to anchor the affirmations with more power and intensity. Thus, it helps us to believe and act on them with greater resolve.

Emotions help to strengthen the mind-body connection.

Written

Writing affirmations down helps to create a deeper connection between your thoughts and your physical actions. In a sense, it is also symbolic. If you do not value affirmations enough to take the time to write them down, then they are not personal enough.

It is important to write the affirmation and not simply type them on a computer. By writing down your affirmations, you are creating a tangible reminder of your goals and intentions. Additionally, writing down affirmations can help to solidify them in your mind, making them easier to remember and recall when you need them.

Affirmations should be repeated with the exact same words for consistency to imprint the message in your brain. Consistency ensures that the message does not confuse the subconscious brain. It is important to remember that actually writing with a pen links the affirmation to your brain through the sense of touch, one of the elements of the human keyboard.

Spoken aloud

When we speak affirmations aloud, we are sending a powerful message to our subconscious mind that we are worthy and capable of achieving our goals. It also helps to boost our self-confidence and self-esteem, as we are actively affirming our worth and potential. Speaking affirmations aloud also helps to create a positive environment and energy around us, which can help to attract more positive experiences into our lives.

Speaking aloud engages your hearing and resonates in your cranial bones, thus increasing the transmission of the message to your brain. The more senses are involved in your affirmation, the stronger the rewiring will be in your subconscious brain.

The power of words

Words have the power to shape our lives and the world around us. They can be used to influence, inspire, inform, and even heal. The impact of words can be felt on many distinct levels creating positive change and bringing people together, or they can be used to divide and incite conflict. The power of words is immense, and it should not be underestimated. By using words wisely, we can make a lasting impact on our lives and the lives of others.

The book of proverbs, which contains nuggets of wisdom from King Solomon, offers many insights into the power of our words. You can almost open this book at random and will find a passage on the importance of guarding your words.

> *"Death and life are in the power of the*
> ``*tongue: and they that love it shall eat the fruit thereof."*
> **Proverbs 18:21**

As indicated previously, words constitute only 7% of the message in business communication when the listener receives the message. From a leadership perspective, if you are influencing one hundred people the impact of this 7% multiplied times the number of people cannot be ignored.

Having said this, the speaker or sender is massively impacted by the spoken words. You would ask Why?
Here is why. When words are spoken, the whole auditory apparatus of the speaker (cranial bone, ears, tongue, and brain manufacturing the thought) is engaged and leaves a mark. The impact is massive as the words spoken express the thought of the sender. Indeed, words are impactful, BUT mostly for the speaker, and not so much for the listener.

Activate, Relax, Affirm, and Visualize

Characterizing words

Words can bring thought and ideas into reality once spoken and can be characterized as seeds. When you plant seeds, you do not know exactly which one will grow, when it will grow, or how tall it will grow exactly. What you have the authority to do is to plant and nurture the seeds to help them grow.

The seed has the authority to grow. If you plant a strawberry seed, it has the authority to grow into a strawberry plant to produce strawberries. You do know that you will not get bananas by planting a strawberry seed. In the same way, words have the authority to grow. If you plant good seeds, they will grow and do good. If you plant bad seeds, they will provide bad fruit.

As a Christian, I am inspired by a letter from Peter who refers to the word of God as an incorruptible seed.

> *"Being born again, not of corruptible seed, but of incorruptible, by the word of God, which liveth and abideth for ever."*
> **Peter 1:23**

Planting seeds

The words of your mouth are related to the thoughts in your mind. Think about the importance of your words and their impact on your surroundings. Just as a farmer selects where he plants his seeds, you need to choose the right environment for your words if you want them to have maximum impact.

You will want to nurture the ideas that you planted to allow them to grow and remove obstacles that will hinder their growth. Be patient, the seeds that you planted will grow on their own time.

Farmers act on faith that their seeds will grow. While not all seeds will grow, they have faith that enough seeds will grow to

Activate, Relax, Affirm, and Visualize

provide the results that they want. You will not see a farmer pull out the seeds to check if they are growing. In the same way, do not kick at the seeds, pull them out, or quit before they have had a chance to grow.

Finally, do not mix the seeds. If you want a crop of strawberries, do not mix strawberry seeds with corn seeds and tomato seeds otherwise you will not be able to collect the fruit of your labor. Your words must be consistent.

This is why having a vision is such an important part for a higher performance as it provides a focus point for your thoughts and words to be aligned towards getting optimal results. As a leader, speak about your goals and help your team to focus on a high-level vision.

The five levels of self-talk

According to Shad Helmstetter, there are five levels of self-talk with the first two lower levels holding people back and the higher levels unleashing their inner power. Recognizing the language that we use in this context allows us to improve our communication with ourselves and with others towards reaching peak performance™.

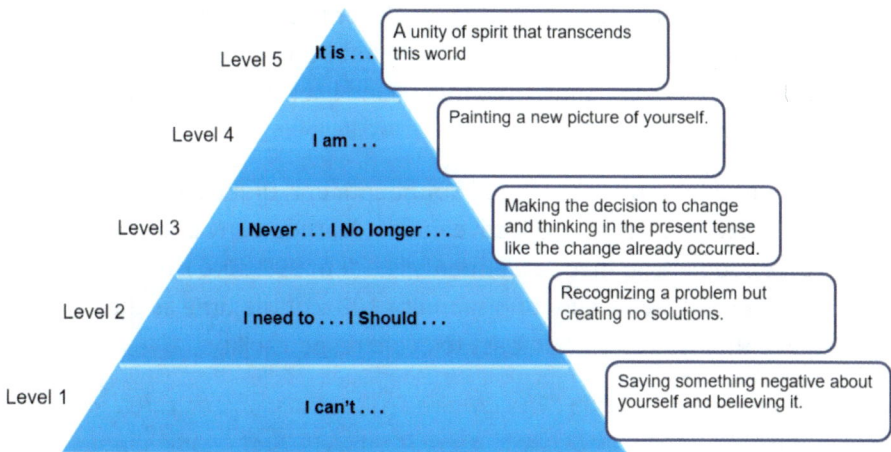

Level 5 — **It is . . .** — A unity of spirit that transcends this world

Level 4 — **I am . . .** — Painting a new picture of yourself.

Level 3 — **I Never . . . I No longer . . .** — Making the decision to change and thinking in the present tense like the change already occurred.

Level 2 — **I need to . . . I Should . . .** — Recognizing a problem but creating no solutions.

Level 1 — **I can't . . .** — Saying something negative about yourself and believing it.

In addition to being positive, personal, and present, affirmations should reflect language at the fourth level of self-talk and paint a new picture of yourself. [33]

Remove limiters

Speed limiters are devices that are usually installed in large trucks to limit the maximum speed at which they can travel. They are typically used to ensure that drivers do not exceed a specific speed. Speed limiters can be used to help reduce the risk of accidents.

_____

[33] Helmstetter, S. (2017). What to say when you talk to your self. Simon and Schuster.

Activate, Relax, Affirm, and Visualize

Fear can be defined as false evidence appearing real on the basis that most of our fears never materialize. Words that propagate fear function as a speed limiter. There is nothing that will slow things down faster than injecting words of fear as it creates confusion. The subconscious brain will notice fear language and raise more questions which creates doubt and confusion instead of focusing on the objective.

Listen to people talk about their goals for five minutes and you will know immediately when they do not honestly believe in the goal. They will use sentences that sound like: "We will try. . .", "we hope. . .", . . .

Do not inject words that seed doubt and fear, or let such words infiltrate your team's collective mind. I learned early in business that people who made statements like "I'm 99% sure that I will be present", were sure to disappoint 100% of the time as they gave themselves 1% as a pass to avoid responsibility.

In the Star Wars film "The Empire Strikes Back", Yoda tells Luke Skywalker, "Do, or Do Not. There is no try." That lesson should play out any time you hear someone say "try."

> **For a period of two years, I accepted all invitation to explore new business opportunities. I witnessed many presentations and observed how people who had managed to remove limiting language attracted crowds. They communicated a clear vision and spoke with absence of fear or doubt.**
>
> **They found a following no matter if the opportunity they showed was legitimate or not. Some had questionable claims citing their friend from a distant place as an authority. Still, people would join them in their quest.**

Activate, Relax, Affirm, and Visualize

Here are five expressions that will limit your speed and the enabling language that you can use to replace them.

Limiting language	Enabling language
If we achieve our goal. . .	When we achieve our goal. . .
I think we can. . .	We can. . .
I am 99% sure that. . .	I am confident that. . .
I have a small project . . .	I have a project . . .
I will try. . .	I will do. . .
I need. . .	I want. . .

We are not proposing that you should lie to yourself if you do not believe that you can accomplish something. Rather, you should be ready to have a fierce conversation to address and resolve the conflict within. A fierce conversation is one in which we come out from behind ourselves into the conversation and make it real. [34]

What are you pretending that you do not know? Address it promptly, positively and forcefully. Decisiveness is key.

Avoiding a conversation eventually leads to a situation where we are then forced to address the conflict which is usually at the wrong time.

From Necessity to Possibilities
The words that we use and the way we phrase things have a direct implication on our subconscious. We want to refrain ourselves from using words about needing things and focus our

---

[34] Scott, S. (2004). Fierce Conversations, Achieving Success at Work & in Life, One Conversation at a time. The Berkley publishing group.

Activate, Relax, Affirm, and Visualize

words and our energy on the things we want. Speaking of what we need suggests a "lack of" and is uninspiring.

There is only one thing we need at this moment. . . Air. The rest we simply want.

Speaking about our wants focuses our attention on possibilities and allows us to break the barrier beyond necessities. By speaking of our wants, we project a sense that we have control over our needs. This positions us in a better place to inspire with a focus on positives and a desire for improvement.

Is there a place for necessity language? Certainly.

If your house is on fire, then "you need water."

Having said this, how often is your house burning? When leaders overuse necessity language, the people receiving the message become complacent to it and the sense of urgency is lost.

We all remember the story of the boy who cried wolf, don't we?

Activate, Relax, Affirm, and Visualize

Visualize

The mental gym is an important concept to create mastery. It requires practicing your mind to visualize the results that you want.

Canadian swimmer and gold medalist Mark Tewksbury described how he was not allowed to visit the Olympic pool while he was traveling to Barcelona because it was under construction. He managed to make his way to the pool area to visualize himself winning the gold medal and the rest was history.

The circle of performance

An effective tool to a higher performance is the circle of performance. Imagine yourself winning and achieving your goals. Add affirmations and emotions into it and you are on your way to succeed.

Imagine a circle on the ground that contains these emotions. Step into the circle and feel the energy . . . Step out when you are at a peak intensity as if you were Muhammad Ali winning your fight against Sonny Liston.

Activate, Relax, Affirm, and Visualize

With practice you will visualize the circle at will and step into it to immediately get back in a state of high energy. I have conditioned myself to it and am feeling high energy just writing about it.

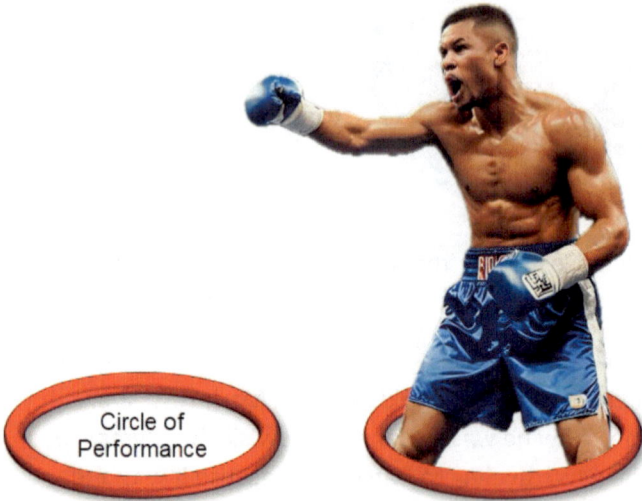

Circle of Performance

Visualization exercises are meant to reach our subconscious mind to instruct it of the desired results that we want.

The right amount

When he was a young man, my grandfather used dynamite sticks to remove stumps and clear new land for farming. In the 1990's his neighbor wanted to remove a tree stump from the front yard and my grandfather offered to help.

He managed to get a few dynamite sticks through his contacts without realizing that the power of dynamite sticks today is stronger than the black powder he worked with in the past. To make this story short, the tree stump was obliterated, as well as the front face of his neighbor's house.

Activate, Relax, Affirm, and Visualize

The moral of the story is that too much of the right stuff is not necessarily better.

It is important to limit the visualization exercise to a period of one to two minutes at most because the subconscious mind tires quickly. Too much of a good thing IS a bad thing.

Key take aways

- Acreavis™ provides a structure to help you channel your energy for maximum results.

- Awareness is heightened when you have a strong WHY.

- The AïM™ process will heighten awareness of old paradigms, internalize new ones, integrate them into the routine to achieve mastery.

- Guard yourself from detailitis, excusitis, and procrastination.

- Activate both your mind and body.
  - Your body works better when accelerated.
  - Your brain works better when it is slowed down.

- Words are like seeds with the power to grow.

- Make your affirmations Personal, Present and Positive.

- Visualize your future in your mental gym.
  - 1-2 minutes of visualization at most.

- Integrate Acreavis™ into your daily routine to reach peak performance™.

Go. . .

It's game time!

Now is the time to put it all into practice with Innoptimax™; To Innovate, Optimize and Maximize results.

You now have the tools to program your mind and focus your energy on doing the right things, in the right amount, at the right time™. You have a vision and a mission with a clear set of values to serve as boundaries that will allow you to get to your goals effectively. You understand the elements of leadership that will allow you to lead, influence, and inspire people for a greater cause. You have set smart goals that are personal and under your control.

We will now explore a few approaches that will enable you to inject excellence through continuous improvements for an organizational breakthrough transformation. We provide a brief introduction to create awareness of a few process improvement tactics that will allow you to aim for your aspirations and exceed expectations.

Innoptimax™

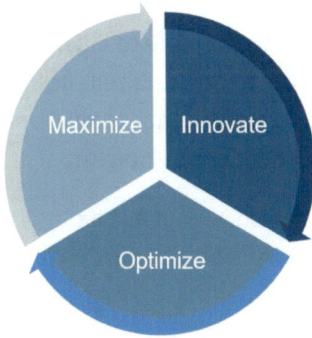

We use the word Innoptimax™ to describe the mindset of excellence based on three actions: to Innovate, to optimize and to maximize. Excellence is a continuous process of challenging ourselves to raise the bar with **INNOVATIVE** ideas and putting them into action to get results that can be **OPTIMIZED** towards **MAXIMIZING** results with Effort-*Less* Effectiveness™. Using the Innoptimax™ process keeps you in a mindset of excellence.

We will provide concepts to keep in mind as you achieve self-transformation and then present a few processes that are tested and proven in the industry. There are many books that explain each process in depth. Our aim is to provide an overview towards creating an awareness. We believe that the implementation of these processes into your daily routine can create a meaningful impact towards instilling excellence.

Achieving a breakthrough transformation

By 2013, Tiger Woods had already achieved seventy-four wins and historic victory margins as well as fourteen majors. His greatest achievement however was the complete reinvention of his game.[35] By 2023 he had eighty-two wins (9 more than Jack Nichlaus) and fifteen majors and has the lowest career scoring average in PGA Tour history. He is a fitting example to illustrate how excellence is a journey and not a destination. Excellence is a state of mind and is fluid. The pursuit of excellence may even require taking a few steps back to advance to new heights.

Excellence is the game; Transformation is the name. The journey to excellence is one of continuous adjustment and transformation.

This implies that keeping to the status quo is not a path to excellence. Transformation can be accelerated with :

1) mentorship,
2) coaching to challenge old paradigms, and
3) the mastermind principle.

The Crab theory

I once learned that if you put a crab in a bucket, it will start to climb out without too much difficulty. When two crabs are placed in a bucket, they will usually fight for dominance. The crabs will use their claws to grab onto each other and attempt to flip the other over. This behavior is known as crab fighting and is a way for the crabs to establish a hierarchy.

In the wild, the crab that can maintain dominance will usually be the one that gets the most food and the best shelter. If the

---

[35] Eden, S. (2013, January 22). Tiger Woods reinvents his golf swing for the third time in his career - ESPN The Magazine - ESPN. ESPN.com. https://www.espn.com/golf/story/_/id/8865487/tiger-woods-reinvents-golf-swing-third-career-espn-magazine

crabs are not separated, they may continue fighting for a lengthy period and can even cause injury to each other.

The moment you add another crab in the bucket, one crab will pull the other back in, ensuring the group's collective demise. [36] [37] [38]

The story is often used as a theory in human behavior which states that members of a group will attempt to reduce the self-confidence of any member who achieves success beyond the others.

---

[36] Low, R. B. P. (2016). Good Intentions Are Not Enough: Why We Fail At Helping Others. World Scientific.

[37] Sarangi, S. (2013). "Capturing Indian 'Crab' Behaviour". The Hindu.

[38] Miller, C. D. (2015). A phenomenological analysis of the crabs in the barrel syndrome. Proceedings - Academy of Management.
https://doi.org/10.5465/ambpp.2015.13710abstract

Dressing for the part
People discriminate. . . Now. . . I have said it.

One of the problems with the word "discrimination" is that it has two definitions. It can represent the unjust or prejudicial treatment of various categories of people, especially on the grounds of ethnicity, age, sex, or disability. It can also represent the recognition and understanding of the difference between one thing and another. The context of how I use the word discrimination is from the latter definition.

You will recall that one of the seven paradigm shifts to peak performance is to transition from judging to evaluating. In a sense, we are continuously judged and evaluated by people. Because of this, we want to show ourselves in the best light to relate with others. It is quite simple, the probability of getting that next opportunity is greater when you communicate in a language that corresponds to the opportunity.

An article in Psychology Today suggests that 93% of all communication is non-verbal. [39] [40]

Research started in 1957 by Albert Mehrabian and duplicated many times since then, has categorized business communications as follows: gestures and appearance give 55% of the message; vocal speed, intonation, pitch, pause, etc. count toward 38% of the message. A mere 7% is carried by words. You will do well if you observe and listen with your eyes.

---

[39] Luna, T. (2020). The Body Language Myth. Is 93% of all communication really nonverbal?"
https://www.psychologytoday.com/us/blog/surprise/202003/the-body-language-myth
[40] Mehrabian, A., & Wiener, M. (1967). Decoding of inconsistent communications. Journal of Personality and Social Psychology, 6(1), 109–114. https://doi.org/10.1037/h0024532

It is worth taking note of your environment and asking yourself if you want to stand out and make a statement, or join in and relate. It is a choice, and the quality of your decision will depend on your goals.

How we dress and express ourselves plays a significant role in how we relate to others and will open or close opportunities. Whether it is fair or not is not the question here. It is a truth that when you go to an interview, are interacting with people who are at a different socio-economic level than you are, are in a different environment than you are used too, you are being evaluated and compared and have a role to play in making this a positive or negative experience.

The old adage says: "Dress for the part that you want".

Learning from others

One method of progressing is through trial and error and applying corrections to gain our own experience. This takes time and effort and will get you to your destination with self-belief.

You can accelerate the process by learning from other people's mistakes. Results will be achieved faster with a feedback loop or follow-up process to inform you if you are applying new concepts effectively or not. Choosing a mentor or hiring a coach will not only provide an opportunity for feedback but also hold you accountable for yourself.

The greatest investment that you can make is an investment in yourself. The ROI (return on investment) is GUARANTEED.

Reading

Reading is an effective way to learn from other people's experience. There are countless books on diverse topics that teach us how to do things if we desire to learn. When I was a teenager, I challenged myself to read our encyclopedia. I read all books from letters "A" through "M" by the time I hit university. Nowadays we have Reddit, Wikipedia, google scholar, YouTube, . . . There is no shortage of resources to learn from.

Most people do not invest enough time in their education after they finish their schooling. They aspire to succeed but do not take the time to read to hone their skills on a topic of interest. My mentor, André Blanchard, would ask "Do you like to read?" If you answered with a "No.," he would say "Read anyways." And then suggest a good book. I recommend "The Go-getter" by Peter Kyne as a starter.

The concept that I learned from André is that if you read 15 minutes per day it is the equivalent of one book per month. At the end of a year it makes 12 books and after 10 years, 120 books which is more than you would read in any university program.

You can expect extraordinary results when you commit to your own development. Coaching and mentorship are a two-way street that requires a commitment from everyone involved. It is not a contract where the coach puts 50% and the coachee puts in 50%. Coaching is a covenant with 100% being given from both parties. Make sure that you follow through with action on the commitments you make.

Mentorship

Experience informs me that people who have already stepped out of the bucket (see the crab theory) want to show you the way out of it and assist you in avoiding their mistakes. These are the mentors, coaches, guides, and advisors who can help you recognize the old mental programs that are preventing you from advancing. They can help you progress from unconscious incompetence to unconscious competence.

I play and compose music on my piano. Like playing the piano, you can learn from a book and train yourself to do the mechanics, but you will accelerate your learning with feedback from someone who has more experience as they can not only point out the gaps quickly but more importantly, prevent you from creating bad habits that will be more difficult to eliminate in the future.

If you are seeking a mentor, look for someone who has already stepped out of the bucket (as per the crab theory) and is living the lifestyle that you are seeking. Check the fruit in the tree to make sure that your mentor is bearing good fruit. A bad tree will not bear good fruit. You should identify people who are not in your management team so that you can confide in them honestly without fear of losing your job.

That is not to say that you shouldn't have a member of the management team being an advocate for you to progress in your career, but rather to state that a mentor will be able to see the forest from the trees and you will not be in a conflict between duty to the company over your duty to yourself and family.

Coaching
A good coach will hold you accountable to yourself. One of the duties of a good coach is to help you see what you may not see in yourself. They will show you how to breakthrough the paradigms that are holding you back. I recommend a coach who has been through the ropes, believes in your abilities, and can help you recognize and realize your potential.

I chose Coach P as my coach and mentor because he has professional experiences that are similar to my own. I was also interested in his experience as an entrepreneur and his positive outlook. More importantly, I could tell that he believed in my abilities to succeed and had a genuine interest in my success.

Coach P introduced me to the elements of his AïM for Life Mastery™ program decades ago and has continued to refine his art over the years with professional athletes and business leaders [41]. Using the concepts of his approach has allowed me to develop and enjoy a career that could be enviable, and I feel blessed by it.

Potential clients often ask, "What will be the deliverable from your coaching proposal?" I will take the time to learn about you and your desires, provide answers based on my experiences, research topics based on your needs, assess, and recommend pathways to accelerate results and reach your goals, and hold you accountable to your potential. As a coachee you will have a structure with space and time dedicated for you to reflect, reach a higher level of awareness of your limiting beliefs, and explore strategies and ideas in a setting that is safe.

A coach's goal and duty is to help you navigate and accelerate the learning curve to reach your vision.

A personal coaching moment
In 2022 I reached out to Coach P to inform him of the abrupt end of my relationship with my employer of 23 years. He helped me realize that I was in a state of unconscious

---

[41] Perras, R. (2011). AïM for Life Mastery™: A Process That Will Empower You to Create Your Chosen Level of Performance While Reducing Stress.

pessimism. He recommended that I write a thank you letter to keep my mind focused on positives during the transition.

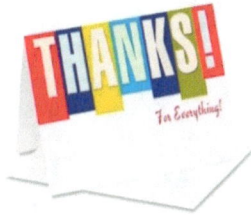

> **Writing A thank you letter will focus your attention on positives.**
>
> **The mind goes to your focus.**

I wrote a four-page letter that clearly expressed how I was thankful for the opportunity of moving from Canada to the United-States for greater opportunities. My last employer sponsored our green cards, my MBA, and other professional training. I made great friends over the years, . . .

Your mind goes to your focus. Taking the time to focus on positives and write down your thoughts will quickly keep you in the right space.

I slept well the following night. The advice was priceless. How many weeks would it have taken to sleep well if not for the "Thank you" letter.

I soon concluded that I wanted to leave corporate America, and start my own business instead of looking for another job. I would build my own business which I fittingly called "SJ Performance, LLC". Essentially, it is Me Inc. expressing my vision, aspirations, values and beliefs.

The guidance from my mentors has been invaluable in distinguishing the forest from the trees. The life experiences I went through over the years have enabled me to provide guidance to people who are seeking to overcome and succeed in reaching their goals.

Man on a cliff.

A man fell from a cliff and was able to cling to a root sticking out a few feet from the top of the cliff.

Man: "Is anyone up there?"
God: "Yes"
Man: "Please help me!"
God: "Do you have faith?
Man: "Yes"
God: "Let go the branch."
Man: "Is there anyone else up there?

This story reminds us how sometimes we forget that we have everything we need to succeed. By not being mindful, intentional, and present, we miss opportunities that might bring massive results (remember the MIP™).

The mastermind Principle

A mastermind group is a fantastic way to accelerate the learning curve with feedback from people who share common goals and have various levels of experience.

In his book "Think and Grow Rich" Napoleon Hill wrote a chapter on the concept of the mastermind which was used by Andrew Carnegie. [42] The Mastermind consist in two or more people actively engaged in the pursuit of a definite purpose with a positive mental attitude. It constitutes an unbeatable force to move forward.

The mastermind principle encourages individuals to reflect on their own strengths and weaknesses, allowing them to become more self-aware and identify areas for improvement. By working with a group of like-minded individuals, they can benefit from the collective wisdom of the group to brainstorm solutions and make more informed decisions.

The mastermind principle provides a supportive environment where individuals can share their ideas and be encouraged to act. It can help individuals gain greater confidence in their own abilities and in their ability to achieve their goals. By working with a group of individuals, each member can expand their network and gain access to novel resources and opportunities with increased motivation and inspiration to reach their goals.

---

[42] Hill, N. (2016). Think and grow rich: The Original, an Official Publication of the Napoleon Hill Foundation.

Practice

I learned through the chemical engineering program that for each action there is a reaction. Successful people do not get there by accident. What lies behind their success is a hidden and often unpopular word called "Work."

The pianist

A woman meeting a professional piano player at the end of the concert and expressed "How I would give my life to play like you do. "

- "This is what I have done." He replied.[43]

There are people of incredible talent and child prodigies like Wolfgang Amadeus Mozart who was composing music at the age of five with his father writing it down on paper. [44] Generally speaking, talent itself is not enough and even Mozart had to continue to work at his skill and eventually learn to write music to put his more than 800 musical works on paper.

Professional musicians do not simply pick up a guitar or sit at a piano and instantly play at a professional level, nor do professional athletes win a gold medal on their first try. Success is the result of following a structure, creating a strategy to channel your energy in a focused direction towards your goal

---

[43] Blanchard, A. (1992). Your financial freedom through network marketing. Saint-Hubert, Quebec : Éditions Un Monde différent.
[44] Deutsch, O. E. (1966). Mozart: A Documentary Biography. Stanford University Press.

and systematically working on mind and body to accomplish the goals.

People often dismiss the years of efforts behind the success of a person. They tell the successful person how lucky they are instead of congratulating them on a well-deserved victory. When meeting a successful person, do not think for a second that they are simply lucky to be where they are but ask about what was involved in getting there and what would be their number one recommendation to help the next generation.

Success leaves clues and asking successful people how they achieved their success is a better way to get a glimpse at those clues.

Practice does not make perfect, what it does is anchor habits. Therefore, practicing the wrong things will result in anchoring the wrong habits and practicing the right things will anchor the habits that will get you to what you desire, a breakthrough transformation to Effort-*Less* Effectiveness™.

Key take aways

- Be ready for a transformation.
- Understand the crab theory.
- Dress for the part that you want.
- Accelerate results with knowledge from others.
  - Read 15 minutes a day towards self-development.
  - Seek a mentor or coach to hold you accountable and help you recognize paradigms that limit your progress.
  - Learn how to use the mastermind principle.
- Learn and adopt a process improvement method.
- Innoptimax™ - Innovate, Optimize and Maximize

Final words

You have been invited to a Breakthrough Transformation™. Congratulations for taking the first steps to a journey that will touch lives in a positive way and last a lifetime. This journey will help you achieve the habit of Effort-*Less* Effectiveness™.

All the acquired knowledge, skills, experiences, and successes that have brought you to this day are yours to keep forever. They are anchored and serve as the foundation of your possibilities to become the best you can be.

This book has opened windows and doors to a process that will enable you to transform who you are into a better person, one that can really thrive on the challenges that arise on your way to Peak Performance™.

We have shared several new concepts (acronyms) that summarize the actions that will enable and empower your transformation. The goal is to help you easily understand and remember the reference points, apply them, and continuously measure progress so that the new YOU becomes a reality.

Remember! What gets measured gets done.

We have covered the foundation, your internal powers, enabling you to get to a state of excellence with GrativatE™.

We then addressed the MIP™ to remind yourself to become more mindful, intentional, and present with the Acreavis™ framework.

We provided insight into the AïM™ framework to create a new awareness of paradigms that may be limiting your progress, internalize new programs and integrate them into the routine towards mastery.

We provided a glimpse to the Transform*Action*™ framework to achieve a state of Peak Performance™ and Effort-*Less* Effectiveness™ used in our personal coaching practice.

Finally, we presented Innoptimax™ as a continuous improvement process with a few strategies to continue to improve your skills and inspire others to GrativatE™ with you along your strategic journey to Peak Performance™.

Do not be surprised if some of the concepts take what seems to be a longer time to master. Slowing down the brain and visualizing takes practice and effort and typically takes 3 to 4 weeks to begin to see and feel a transformation.

Success is a journey and not a destination. Think bigger, take chances. . . if you fall . . . get back up and learn from the experience and continue moving. The journey to success is not a race but a marathon where success can be compared to the growth of a bamboo tree. You need only to get to the finish line to find out for yourself. You are the architect of your future. The decision is in your hands and no one else's.

We aspire to see you achieve higher goals in the future. Higher than you can think or imagine at present.

We aspire to help you take ownership for your future, embrace gratitude, instill self-belief, and seek excellence.

The Chinese bamboo tree

Bamboos include some of the fastest-growing plants in the world. Certain species can grow three feet within a 24-hour period. However, what appears at the surface can be deceiving.

Like any plant, the bamboo tree requires care – water, healthy soil, and sun. However, the one who planted the tree will not see evidence of life for at least four years. This can leave someone wondering if their efforts to care for this plant are being wasted. One's patience may be tested when the plant fails to sprout after so many years.

In the fifth year of caring for this plant, it will begin to shoot up and grow up to eighty feet within just six weeks. What people will see as instant success is the end results of long-term preparation.

This seeming instant success could not happen without years of nurturing to build the foundation with strong roots to sustain the bamboo tree at full maturity.

You Can Do It!

About Stéphane Joanis

Stéphane has a bachelor's degree in chemical engineering from University of Ottawa, Canada, and a master's in business administration from Robert Morris University.

As a chemical engineer, he developed a new process to improve the quality of high purity selenium. He also simulated heavy water flowing through various fuel bundle configurations for nuclear reactor design. He got published for his contribution in developing a formula to predict pressure drop for ice slurry mixtures moving through pipes.

Stéphane began his journey as a leader when he was 23 years old after the death of his father from pancreatic cancer. Taking the lead, he dedicated the next five years to helping his mother run and grow the business that his parents had started together.

 He began his professional career as a customer service representative for Fisher Scientific in Canada and took on roles of increased responsibility while continuing to support the family business.

In 2006, he and his wife started a new business using relational marketing. In just six months, they grew the business from having no clients to having over 250 clients. That year, he and his wife were recognized among the manufacturer's top ten pacesetter earners.

In 2008, Stéphane decided to focus on his professional career and hired Coach P to help him learn parts of a process that he later came to name Peak Performance™.

In 2011, Stéphane was promoted to senior global strategic pricing analyst for Thermo Fisher Scientific's new corporate global strategic pricing team in Pittsburgh, where he and his family reside today.

In 2013, he was promoted as the senior global strategic pricing analyst of the chemical analysis division, an analytical instrument manufacturing division representing up to five business units and $1 billion in annual revenue.

He harmonized data from a dozen ERP systems into a data warehouse, and then introduced workshops that led to a cultural transformation aligning finance, marketing, sales operations, business development, and commercial teams, to use pricing more strategically.

He recommended prices for the introduction of dozens of new chemical analysis instruments and became a go-to resource for over sixty product managers.

In 2017, he was promoted to product manager and led two product lines for optical safety and security instruments. He captured the voice of customers from around the world to introduce Defender Omega and was also responsible for the addition of low-dose capabilities to Gemini, which enabled US customs and border patrol to identify fentanyl and opioids in lower concentrations.

He completed his MBA in 2018 and subsequently held positions as commercial finance/business intelligence manager and Sr. manager of market intelligence before starting his own business, SJ Performance, LLC.

Stéphane's application of the Peak Performance™ framework during his professional career has helped him to lead breakthrough transformations and contribute to the company's success with new processes that have provided tens of millions in profit through global strategic pricing initiatives, millions in revenue growth with the introduction of multiple new products and product improvements, and millions in productivity improvements through enhanced pricing, business intelligence, and competitive intelligence process efficiencies.

These experiences have helped Stéphane improve his business acumen, enabling him to provide greater value as a coach and advisor for the clients-partners that he now serves.

Lastly, Stéphane enjoys spending time with his family, writing music, and practicing his piano at home. In addition, he relishes talking about pricing tactics, leadership development, and business strategy.

About Raymond Perras (Coach P)

As a professional engineer, an experienced project manager, a certified Professional Coach, a certified Instructor/Facilitator, a certified Life Coach, a certified Agile Scrum Master, a certified NLP Practitioner, and a certified Instant Miracle Master, Raymond brings a unique combination of technology and human potential to the table.

He draws from extensive involvement with Information Technology implementation linked to years of organizational development and leadership coaching to help align on purpose. This leads to an organizational transformation founded on Effort-*Less* Effectiveness™ framed by optimal use of all human resources. The Voice of Customer is a critical factor in enabling the continuous achievement of lofty goals.

Coaching individuals and organizations to peak performance in both business and sports for over twenty-five years, his expertise is the X-factor in bringing it all together in a journey to Peak Performance™.

His coaching provides the framework, the techniques and the practices that enable you to produce a structured, strategic, and systematic approach in your daily routine. You will create peak performance in your life by applying the right stuff, in the right amount, at the right time™ (his definition of peak performance).

Having witnessed the transformation of numerous clients from average to outstanding performers, he shares a unique process to create awareness, internalize and integrate it, and master the knowledge and ability to make it second nature.

Corporate clients for whom he has provided coaching and advisory services include RJR Innovations, ChenMed, Abarca

Excellence through Peak Performance™

Health, Perficient Inc., Woodmen Life, SBC Telecom, State Farm Insurance, Canopy Growth and SJ Performance, LLC. In pro football, he teamed up with Saskatchewan Roughriders and Hamilton Tiger-Cats, and in hockey Quebec Nordiques (now Colorado Avalanche) and Ottawa Senators.

He is a published author and contributor to several books including *AïM for Life Mastery*™, a recipe for peak performance, and *10 Discussions for Effective Leadership*, the application of principles to enhance a leader's effectiveness.

Raymond lives in Ottawa, Ontario, Canada. His performance coaching business offers services to individuals, businesses and sports organizations in Canada, USA and abroad as far as Dubai. He strives to find new ways to increase the value of peak performance for his clients. The end goal is always to seek personal and organizational transformation that produces the best possible results with the least effort while reducing stress.

About SJ Performance, LLC

Our vision is to guide people to self-transformation in becoming heart centered leaders. We accomplish this by enabling our clients to achieve Peak Performance™.

Our high-tech and high-touch approach combines technological know-how and human potential with a focus on excellence. We believe that the greater part of any solution is the execution through people.

Excellence is the name; transformation is the game!

Excellence is not a destination but a state and frame of mind where we continuously seek to innovate and optimize our processes to achieve maximum results and effectiveness.

We are in the business of transformation.

We facilitate the alignment process through a clear and compelling vision and mission. We help to achieve the vision in a way that is structured, strategic, systematic, and scalable. We promote values that allow the flexibility to make decisions while providing guardrails to prevent the organization from wiping out during critical decisive moments.

We believe that peak performance is achieved when the mind and body, conscious and subconscious are aligned with our vision, mission, and values towards Effort-*Less* Effectiveness™.

We believe in the process of discovering and assessing to co-create solutions with our clients in a way that aligns with their culture and uses world-class processes and best practices.

The right stuff, in the right amounts, at the right time™.

Even the best ideas can fail without team alignment. We help our clients develop the conviction that is necessary to move away from their pain and take them through the journey from pain island to pleasure island.

Peak Performance™

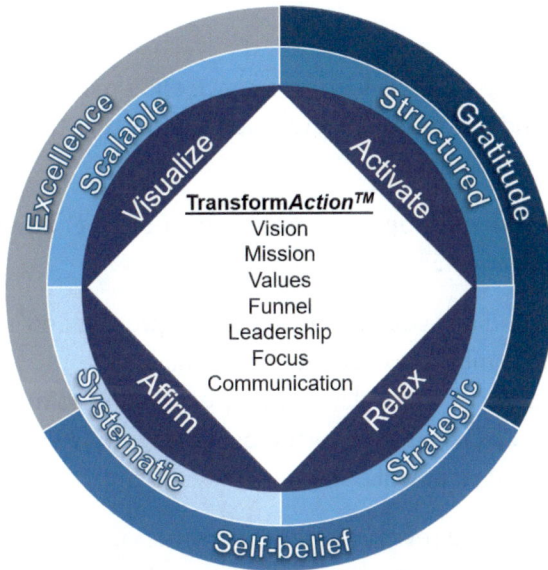

We define peak performance as: "the right stuff, in the right amount, at the right time™."

We partner with your organization to create a breakthrough transformation to new levels of excellence in your professional and personal lives.

We are dedicated to partnering with clients to create a breakthrough transformation in their quest for excellence in business. By combining our technical know-how with our coaching expertise, we help organizations and individuals achieve Effort-*Less* Effectiveness™ while reducing stress. We facilitate the transformation to a team that thrives on change through a strategic, open, and targeted communication process.

The Leadership Think Tank

The leadership think tank offers a space and time for reflection, strategy, and masterminding to instill and nurture the mindset for Peak Performance™.

We begin with developing awareness to your inner powers using the GrativatE™ framework.

On the second day you live the Acreavis™ process and learn to prepare your mind and body for performance. As the program progresses along, you will have many opportunities to experience Spice™ as a powerful tool to re-ground and re-energize yourself at will.

You are invited to revisit your own personal vision, mission, and values towards becoming a more effective leader. We will help you formulate affirmations in a way that pulls your subconscious to be at your service.

On the morning of the final day we focus on visualization and building a heart-centered leadership mind map. We then introduce Innoptimax™ as a continuous improvement framework and explore deployment strategies.

Our goal is to guide you through a strategic journey to a breakthrough transformation to maximize results and minimize stress; a self-transformation in becoming a heart-centered leader.

The Mastermind Principle

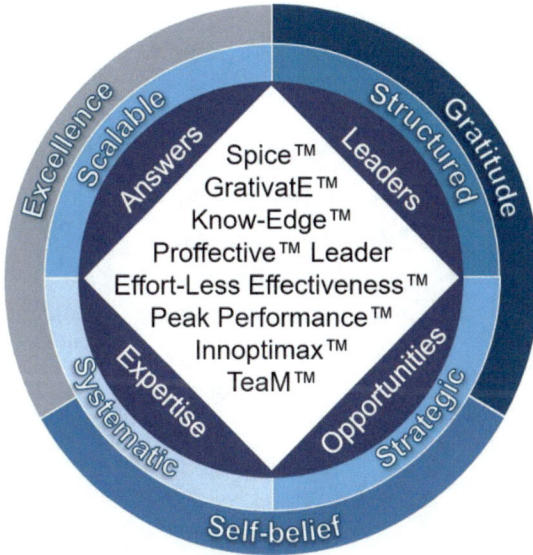

Spice™
GrativatE™
Know-Edge™
Proffective™ Leader
Effort-Less Effectiveness™
Peak Performance™
Innoptimax™
TeaM™

Mastermind groups allow you to tap into the collective knowledge of like-minded people to address your most pressing challenges. No task is too great for a collective mind.

In a mastermind, the participants give each other advice and support. It will only have five or six members and can involve brainstorming, ideation, and discussion on varying topics that are decided by the group. Some people may think of these groups as master classes, but they are not. There is no single teacher with a prepared lesson.

The learning is from the experience of participants who willingly share best practices towards forming a collective mind to reach your goals more efficiently.

Pricing Excellence

We specialize in leading and guiding the cultural transformation necessary to get an organization to effectively implement sustainable value-based pricing processes and will see the strategy through to its deployment with follow up coaching.

We help our clients develop strategies, supported by data, to maximize profit while maintaining trust and consumer confidence. Our insights are built on years of experience helping businesses make important decisions for maximum impact, and minimum risk.

Appendix A – List of favorite books

AïM for Life Mastery, Raymond Perras

The book provides a recipe that will help you to create peak performance™; "the right stuff, in the right amount, at the right time". The key is to work with your best abilities to gain awareness, internalize it in your bag of tricks, integrate it into your daily routine, and practice until it becomes second nature.

Skill with People, Les Giblin

Learn to improve your people skills and your ability to make strong, lasting impressions on the people you meet every day. Skill with people is described as "the most wisdom in the least words". You will learn to listen with sensitivity.

How to win Friends and Influence People, Dale Carnegie

Learn the six ways to make people like you, the twelve ways to win people to your way of thinking, and the nine ways to change people without arousing resentment. This timeless bestseller is packed with rock-solid advice that has carried thousands of now famous people up the ladder of success in their business and personal lives.

What to say when you talk to yourself, Shad Helmstetter

Learn how to reverse the effects of negative self-talk and embrace a more positive, optimistic outlook on life!

Think and Grow Rich, Napoleon Hill

The distilled wisdom of distinguished men of great wealth and achievement. Andrew Carnegie's magic formula for success was the direct inspiration for this book. Carnegie demonstrated its soundness when his coaching brought fortunes to those young men to whom he had disclosed his secret.

The Magic of Thinking Big, David J. Schwartz, PH. D

A carefully designed program for getting the most out of your job, your marriage and family life, and your community. Learn and understand the habit of thinking and behaving in ways that will get you there.

Emotional Intelligence: Why It Can Matter More Than IQ, Daniel Goleman

Offers startling insight into our "two minds"—the rational and the emotional—and how they together shape our destiny. Explore how self-awareness, self-discipline, and empathy can be nurtured and add up to a different way of being smart.

The Go-Getter: A Story That Tells You How to be One, Peter B. Kyne

The tale of a true fighter that has lifted many a salesperson from the rut and set his feet on the road to success.

Failing Forward: Turning Mistakes into Stepping Stones for Success, John C. Maxwell

A strategic guide that will help people move beyond mistakes to fulfill their potential and achieve success. The secret of moving beyond failure is to use it as a lesson and a stepping-stone.

The Speed of Trust, Stephen M.R. Covey

Shows how trust and the speed at which it is established with clients, employees and constituents is the essential ingredient for any high-performance, successful organization.

The Seven Habits of Highly Effective People, Stephen R. Covey

A holistic, integrated, principle-centered approach for solving personal and professional problems. A step-by-step pathway for living with fairness, integrity, honesty, and human dignity— principles that give us the security to adapt to change and the wisdom and power to take advantage of the opportunities that change creates.

The First 90 Days, Proven Strategies for Getting Up to Speed Faster and Smarter, Michael D. Watkins

proven strategies for conquering the challenges of transitions - no matter where you are in your career. Learn how to secure critical early wins, an important first step in establishing yourself in your new role.

The Leadership Challenge, J. M. Kouzes, B.Z. Posner

The premier resource on becoming a leader. "Leadership is Everyone's Business." Learn the "five practices" and "ten commitments" that have been proven by hundreds of thousands of dedicated, successful leaders.

Start with the Why, Simon Sinek

Shows that the leaders who have had the greatest influence in the world all think, act, and communicate the same way—and it's the opposite of what everyone else does. It all starts with WHY.

The Leadership Pipeline, Ram Charan, Stephen Drotter, James Noel

A tested model for planning leadership succession and development that has proven to get results. Learn how a company can develop leadership in each layer of their organization by defining the different skills required as leaders move from one level to the next.

Made in the USA
Thornton, CO
09/09/24 05:43:44